Learn
CSS
with w3schools

**Hege Refsnes, Ståle Refsnes, Kai Jim Refsnes,
and Jan Egil Refsnes
with Joell Smith-Borne**

WILEY
Wiley Publishing, Inc.

Learn CSS with w3schools

Published by
Wiley Publishing, Inc.
111 River Street
Hoboken, NJ 07030-5774
www.wiley.com

Copyright © 2010 by Wiley Publishing, Inc., Indianapolis, Indiana

Published simultaneously in Canada

ISBN: 978-0-470-61192-0

LOC/CIP: 2010924597

Manufactured in the United States of America

10 9 8 7 6 5 4 3 2 1

For general information on our other products and services please contact our Customer Care Department within the United States at (877) 762-2974, outside the United States at (317) 572-3993 or fax (317) 572-4002.

Wiley also publishes its books in a variety of electronic formats. Some content that appears in print may not be available in electronic books.

Library of Congress CIP Data is available from the publisher.

w3schools Authors/Editors

w3schools' mission is to publish well-organized and easy-to-understand online tutorials based on the W3C Web standards.

Hege Refsnes

Hege is a writer and editor for w3schools. She works to improve the usability and accessibility of the Web.

Hege has been writing tutorials for w3schools since 1998.

Ståle Refsnes

Ståle has ten years of Internet development experience, developing all the Web-based solutions for The Norwegian Handball Federation.

Ståle has been writing tutorials for w3schools since 1999.

Kai Jim Refsnes

Kai Jim has been around computers since childhood, working with them since the age of 14.

He has been writing tutorials for w3schools since completing a bachelor's degree in information technology in 2005.

Jan Egil Refsnes

Jan Egil is the president and founder of w3schools.

He is a senior system developer with a master's degree in information technology and more than 30 years of computing experience.

"Jani" has supervised a large number of company critical development projects for oil companies like Amoco, British Petroleum, ELF, Halliburton, and Brown & Root. He has also developed computer-based solutions for more than 20 governmental institutions like The National Library, Norwegian High Schools, The State Hospital, and many others.

Jani started w3schools in 1998.

Credits

Acquisitions Editor
Scott Meyers

Production
Abshier House

Copy Editor
Abshier House

Associate Director of Marketing
David Mayhew

Production Manager
Tim Tate

Vice President and Executive Group Publisher
Richard Swadley

Vice President and Executive Publisher
Barry Pruett

Associate Publisher
Jim Minatel

Project Coordinator, Cover
Lynsey Stanford

Proofreading and Indexing
Abshier House

Cover Designer
Michael Trent

TABLE OF CONTENTS

INTRODUCTION

Welcome to *Learn CSS with w3schools*. This book is for Web site designers and builders who want to learn to design sites using the Web standard CSS. w3schools (www.w3schools.com) is one of the top Web destinations to learn CSS and many other key Web languages. Founded in 1998, w3schools tutorials are recommended reading in more than 100 universities and high schools all over the world. This book is a great companion to the CSS tutorials on the w3schools site. The tutorials were written by Jan Egil Refsnes, Ståle Refsnes, Kai Jim Refsnes, and Hege Refsnes.

Like the w3schools online tutorials, this book features a brief presentation of each topic, trading lengthy explanations for abundant examples showcasing each key feature. This book, as well as other w3schools books published by Wiley, features straightforward and concise tutorials on each topic from which the beginning Web developer can easily learn. All of the book's content is derived from w3schools' accurate, user-tested content used by millions of learners every month.

CSS

Save a lot of work with CSS!

In this book you learn how to use CSS to control the style and layout of multiple Web pages all at once.

What You Should Already Know

Before you continue, you should have a basic understanding of HTML/XHTML.

If you want to study these subjects first, please read *Learn HTML and CSS with w3schools*.

What Is CSS?

▸▸ **CSS** stands for **C**ascading **S**tyle **S**heets.

▸▸ Styles define **how to display** HTML elements.

▸▸ Styles were added to HTML 4.0 **to solve a problem**.

▸▸ **External Style Sheets** can save a lot of work.

▸▸ External Style Sheets are stored in **CSS files**.

CSS Demo

An HTML document can be displayed with different styles. Figure I.1 shows a Web page with no styles attached, while Figure I.2 and Figure I.3 show the same Web page with different styles applied.

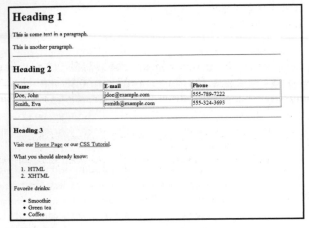

Figure I.1

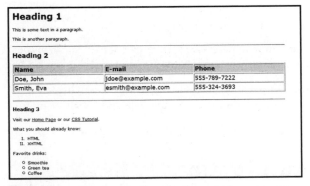

Figure I.2

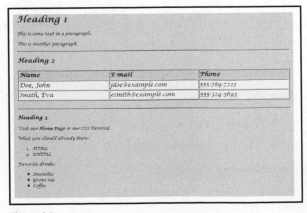

Figure I.3

Styles Solved a Big Problem

HTML was never intended to contain tags for formatting a document.

HTML was intended to define the content of a document, like:

```
<h1>This is a heading</h1>
<p>This is a paragraph.</p>
```

When tags like `<font>` and color attributes were added to the HTML 3.2 specification, it started a nightmare for Web developers. Development of large Web sites, where fonts and color information were added to each individual page, became a long and expensive process.

To solve this problem, the World Wide Web Consortium (W3C) created CSS.

In HTML 4.0, all formatting could be removed from the HTML document and stored in a separate CSS file.

All browsers support CSS today.

CSS Saves a Lot of Work!

CSS defines **how** HTML elements are to be displayed.

Styles are normally saved in external .css files. External style sheets enable you to change the appearance and layout of all the pages on a Web site just by editing one file!

Here are the style sheets for the page shown at the beginning of this chapter:

Style 1 style sheet:

```
body
{
  font-size:75%;
  font-family:verdana,arial,'sans serif';
  background-color:#FFFFF0;
  color:#000080;
  margin:10px;
}

h1 {font-size:200%;}
h2 {font-size:140%;}
h3 {font-size:110%;}

th {background-color:#ADD8E6;}

ul {list-style:circle;}
```

```
ol {list-style:upper-roman;}

a:link {color:#000080;}
a:hover {color:red;}
```

Style 2 style sheet:

```
body
{
  font-size:75%;
  font-family:"lucida calligraphy",arial,'sans serif';
  background-color:#DCDCDC;
  color:#8A2BE2;
  margin:10px;
}

h1 {font-size:200%;}
h2 {font-size:140%;}
h3 {font-size:110%;}

th {background-color:#D3D3D3;}
td {background-color:#FFFAF0;}

a:link {color:#8A2BE2;text-decoration:none;}
a:hover {color:red;font-weight:bold;text-decoration:none;}
a:visited {text-decoration:none;}
```

How To Use This Book

Throughout this book, you will see several icons:

Try it yourself >>

The Try it yourself icon indicates an opportunity for you to practice what you've just learned. The code and examples under this icon come from examples on the w3schools site, which allow you to make changes to the code and see the results immediately. You do not have to type the code examples in this book; you can find them all on the w3schools site.

The w3schools icon indicates that more information is available on the w3schools site.

This icon indicates where you will find further information about a topic that is covered more thoroughly elsewhere within the book.

NOTE Notes provide important cautions and information about making sure your code will work in all browsers.

TIP Tips give you hints to make coding easier.

This book is divided into six sections and a set of useful appendixes:

Section I: CSS Basic

Section II: CSS Styling

Section III: CSS Box Model

Section IV: CSS Layout

Section V: CSS Advanced

Section VI: Conclusion

Appendixes: CSS Reference Guides

If you're anxious to improve your Web pages and to add some interactivity, jump right in with "CSS Basic." Plenty of examples and opportunities to try things await, but w3schools will be right there when you need them.

Section I
CSS Basic

CHAPTER 1

CSS SYNTAX

A CSS rule has two main parts: a **selector** and one or more **declarations.**

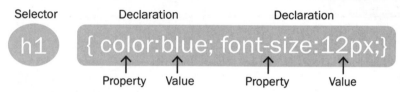

The **selector** is normally the HTML element you want to style.

Each **declaration** consists of a **property** and a **value**.

The **property** is the style attribute you want to change. Each property has a **value**.

CSS Example

CSS declarations always end with a semicolon, and declaration groups are surrounded by curly brackets:

```
p {color:red;text-align:center}
```

To make the CSS more readable, you can put one declaration on each line, like this:

```
p
{
  color:red;
  text-align:center;
}
```

The result of this code is shown in Figure 1.1.

Try it yourself >>

```
<html>
<head>
<style type="text/css">
  p
  {
```

(continued)

9

(continued)

```
      color:red;
      text-align:center;
  }
</style>
</head>

<body>
<p>Hello World!</p>
<p>This paragraph is styled with CSS.</p>
</body>
</html>
```

Hello World!

This paragraph is styled with CSS.

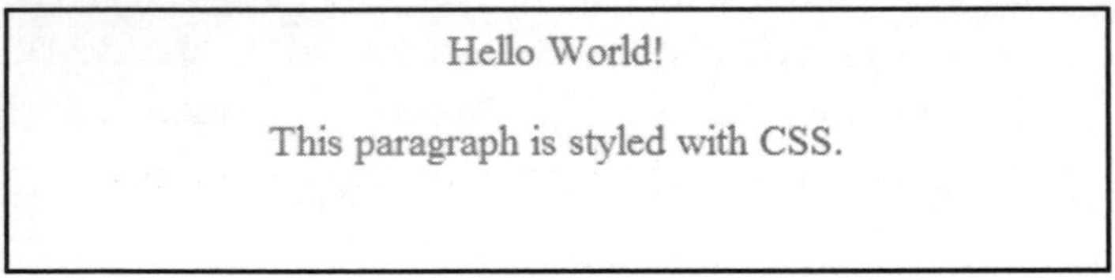

Figure 1.1

CSS Comments

Comments are used to explain your code and may help you when you edit the source code at a later date. Comments are ignored by browsers.

A CSS comment begins with /* and ends with */, like this:

```
/*This is a comment*/
p
{
  text-align:center;
  /*This is another comment*/
  color:black;
  font-family:arial
}
```

Style Sheet Examples

This HTML file links to an external style sheet with the <link> tag. The result of this code is shown in Figure 1.2.

```
<html>
<head>
<link rel="stylesheet"
type="text/css" href="ex1.css" />
</head>

<body>

<h1>This header is 36 pt</h1>
<h2>This header is blue</h2>

<p>This paragraph has a left margin of 50 pixels</p>

</body>
</html>
```

This is the style sheet file (ex1.css):

```
body
{
   background-color:yellow;
}
h1
{
   font-size:36pt;
}
h2
{
   color:blue;
}
p
{
   margin-left:50px;
}
```

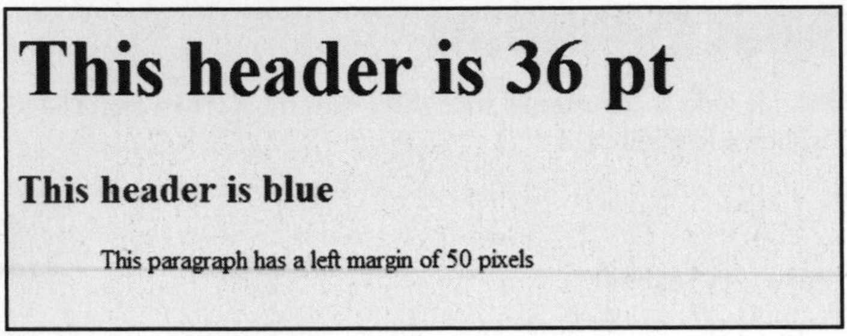

This header is 36 pt

This header is blue

This paragraph has a left margin of 50 pixels

Figure 1.2

This HTML file also links to an external style sheet with the <link> tag. The result of this code is shown in Figure 1.3.

```
<html>
<head>
<link rel="stylesheet" type="text/css"
href="ex2.css" />
</head>

<body>

<h1>This is a header 1</h1>
<hr />

<p>You can see that the style
sheet formats the text</p>

<p><a href="http://www.w3schools.com"
target="_blank">This is a link</a></p>

</body>
</html>
```

This is the style sheet file (ex2.css):

```
body {background-color: tan}
h1 {color:maroon; font-size:20pt}
hr {color:navy}
p {font-size:11pt; margin-left: 15px}
a:link    {color:green}
a:visited {color:yellow}
```

```
a:hover      {color:black}
a:active     {color:blue}
```

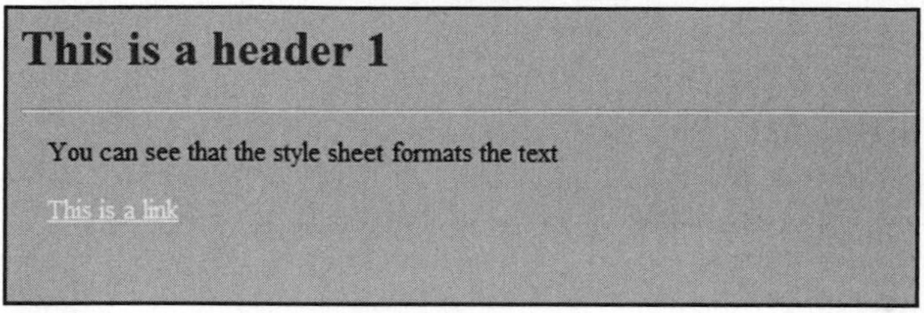

> # This is a header 1
>
> You can see that the style sheet formats the text
>
> This is a link

Figure 1.3

CHAPTER 2

CSS ID AND CLASS

In addition to setting a style for an HTML element, CSS allows you to specify your own selectors called id and class.

The id Selector

The id selector is used to specify a style for a single, unique element.

The id selector uses the id attribute of the HTML element and is defined with a #.

The style rule that follows will be applied to the element with id=para1:

```
#para1
{
    text-align:center;
    color:red
}
```

The result of this code is shown in Figure 2.1.

N O T E Do *not* start an id name with a number! It will not work in Mozilla/Firefox.

Try it yourself >>

```
<html>
<head>
<style type="text/css">
  #para1
  {
    text-align:center;
    color:red
```

```
    }
  </style>
</head>

<body>
<p id="para1">Hello World!</p>
<p>This paragraph is not affected by the style.</p>
</body>
</html>
```

```
                    Hello World!

This paragraph is not affected by the style.
```

Figure 2.1

The class Selector

The class selector is used to specify a style for a group of elements. Unlike the id selector, the class selector is most often used on several elements.

This allows you to set a particular style for any HTML elements with the same class.

The class selector uses the HTML class attribute and is defined with a ".".

In the following example, shown in Figure 2.3, all HTML elements with class=center will be center-aligned:

```
.center {text-align:center}
```

Try it yourself >>

```
<html>
<head>
<style type="text/css">
  .center
  {
    text-align:center;
  }
</style>
</head>
```

(continued)

(continued)

```
<body>
<h1 class="center">Center-Aligned Heading</h1>
<p class="center">Center-aligned paragraph.</p>
</body>
</html>
```

Center-Aligned Heading

Center-aligned paragraph.

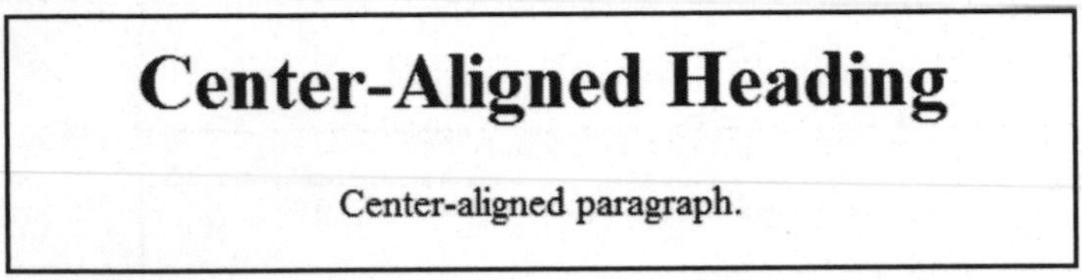

Figure 2.2

You can also specify that only specific HTML elements should be affected by a class.

In the following example, shown in Figure 2.3, all p elements with `class=center` will be center-aligned:

N O T E Do **not** start a class name with a number! This is only supported in Internet Explorer.

```
p.center {text-align:center}
```

Try it yourself >>

```
<html>
<head>
<style type="text/css">
  p.center
  {
    text-align:center;
  }
</style>
</head>

<body>
<h1 class="center">This heading will not be affected</h1>
<p class="center">This paragraph will be center-aligned.</p>
```

```
</body>
</html>
```

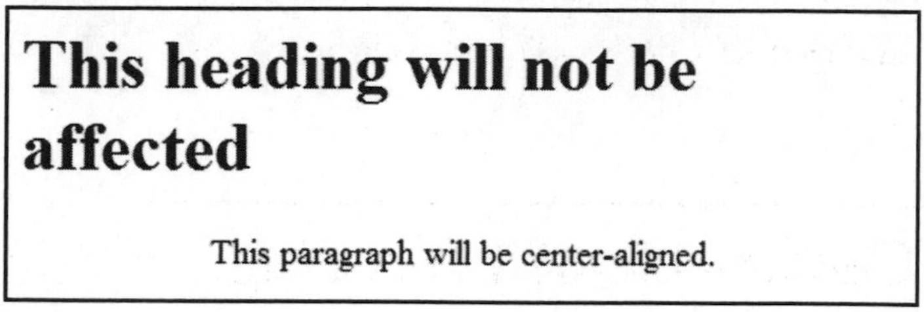

This heading will not be affected

This paragraph will be center-aligned.

Figure 2.3

CHAPTER 3

CSS HOW TO...

When a browser reads a style sheet, it formats the document according to that style sheet.

Three Ways to Insert CSS

There are three ways of inserting a style sheet:

▸▸ External style sheet

▸▸ Internal style sheet

▸▸ Inline style

External Style Sheet

An external style sheet is ideal when the style is applied to many pages. With an external style sheet, you can change the look of an entire Web site by changing one file. Each page must link to the style sheet using the `<link>` tag. The `<link>` tag goes inside the head section:

```
<head>
<link rel="stylesheet" type="text/css" href="mystyle.css" />
</head>
```

An external style sheet can be written in any text editor. The file should not contain any HTML tags. Your style sheet should be saved with a .css extension. The following is an example of a style sheet file:

```
hr {color:sienna}
p {margin-left:20px}
body {background-image:url("images/back40.gif")}
```

> **NOTE** Do not leave spaces between the property value and the units! `margin-left:20 px` (instead of `margin-left:20px`) will work in IE, but not in Firefox or Opera.

Internal Style Sheet

An internal style sheet should be used when a single document has a unique style. You define internal styles in the head section of an HTML page by using the <style> tag, like this:

```
<head>
<style type="text/css">
  hr {color:sienna}
  p {margin-left:20px}
  body {background-image:url("images/back40.gif")}
</style>
</head>
```

Inline Styles

An inline style loses many of the advantages of style sheets by mixing content with presentation. Use this method sparingly!

To use inline styles you use the `style` attribute in the relevant tag. The `style` attribute can contain any CSS property. This example shows how to change the color and the left margin of a paragraph:

```
<p style="color:sienna;margin-left:20px">This is a
   paragraph.</p>
```

Multiple Style Sheets

If some properties have been set for the same selector in different style sheets, the values will be inherited from the more specific style sheet.

For example, an external style sheet has these properties for the h3 selector:

```
h3
{
  color:red;
  text-align:left;
  font-size:8pt
}
```

And an internal style sheet has these properties for the h3 selector:

```
h3
{
    text-align:right;
    font-size:20pt
}
```

If the page with the internal style sheet also links to the external style sheet, the properties for h3 will be:

```
color:red;
text-align:right;
font-size:20pt
```

The color is inherited from the external style sheet, and the text alignment and the font size are replaced by the internal style sheet.

Multiple Styles Will Cascade into One

Styles can be specified

▸▸ inside an HTML element.

▸▸ inside the head section of an HTML page.

▸▸ in an external CSS file.

TIP Even multiple external style sheets can be referenced inside a single HTML document.

Cascading Order

What style will be used when there is more than one style specified for an HTML element?

Generally speaking, we can say that all the styles will "cascade" into a new "virtual" style sheet by the following rules, where number four has the highest priority:

1. Browser default

2. External style sheet

3. Internal style sheet (in the head section)

4. Inline style (inside an HTML element)

So, an inline style (inside an HTML element) has the highest priority, which means that it will override a style defined inside the <head> tag, or in an external style sheet, or in a browser (a default value).

> **N O T E** If the link to the external style sheet is placed after the internal style sheet in HTML <head>, the external style sheet will override the internal style sheet!

Section II
CSS Styling

CHAPTER 4

STYLING BACKGROUNDS

CSS background properties are used to define the background effects of an element.

CSS properties used for background effects:

- `background-color`
- `background-image`
- `background-repeat`
- `background-attachment`
- `background-position`

Background Color

The `background-color` property specifies the background color of an element.

The background color of a page is defined in the **body** selector:

    body {background-color:#b0c4de}

The result of this code is shown in Figure 4.1.

Try it yourself >>

```
<html>
<head>
<style type="text/css">
  body
  {
    background-color:#b0c4de;
  }
</style>
</head>
```

(continued)

(continued)

```
    <body>

    <h1>My CSS web page!</h1>
    <p>Hello world! This is a w3schools.com example.</p>

    </body>
    </html>
```

My CSS web page!

Hello world! This is a w3schools.com example.

Figure 4.1

The background color can be specified by:

▸▸ Name—a color name, like `red`

▸▸ RGB—an RGB value, like `rgb(255,0,0)`

▸▸ Hex—a hex value, like `#ff0000`

In the following example, the h1, p, and div elements have different background colors:

```
h1 {background-color:#6495ed}
p {background-color:#e0ffff}
div {background-color:#b0c4de}
```

The result of this code is shown in Figure 4.2.

Try it yourself >>

```
<html>
<head>
<style type="text/css">
  h1
  {
    background-color:#6495ed;
  }
  p
  {
    background-color:#e0ffff;
```

```
   }
   div
   {
     background-color:#b0c4de;
   }
</style>
</head>

<body>

<h1>CSS background-color example!</h1>
<div>
   This is a text inside a div element.
   <p>This paragraph has its own background color.</p>
   We are still in the div element.
</div>

</body>
</html>
```

CSS background-color example!

This is a text inside a div element.

This paragraph has its own background color.

We are still in the div element.

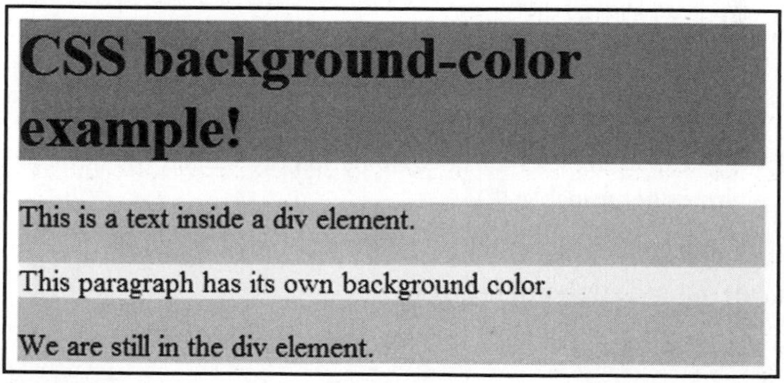

Figure 4.2

Background Image

The background-image property specifies an image to use as the background of an element.

By default, the image is repeated so it covers the entire element.

The background image for a page can be set like this:

```
body {background-image:url('paper.gif')}
```

The result of this code is shown in Figure 4.3.

27

```
<html>
<head>
<style type="text/css">
  body {background-image:url('paper.gif')}
</style>
</head>

<body>
<h1>Hello World!</h1>
</body>

</html>
```

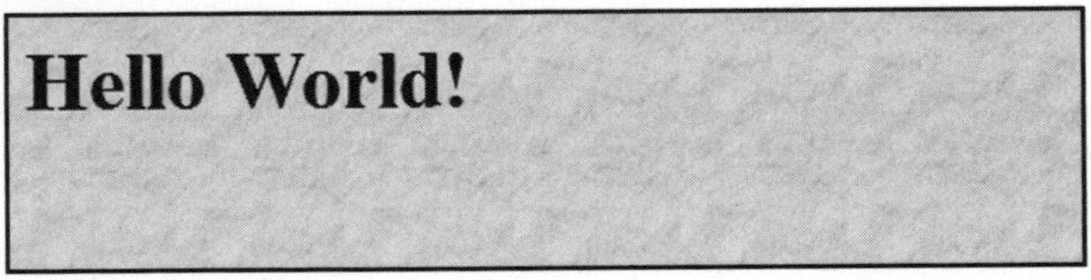

Hello World!

Figure 4.3

The following is an example of a bad combination of text and background image. The text is almost not readable:

```
body {background-image:url('bgdesert.jpg')}
```

The result of this code is shown in Figure 4.4.

```
<html>
<head>
<style type="text/css">
  body
  {
    background-image:url('bgdesert.jpg');
  }
</style>
</head>

<body>
```

```
<h1>Hello World!</h1>
<p>This text is not easy to read on this background image.
   </p>
</body>

</html>
```

Figure 4.4

Background Image—Repeat Horizontally or Vertically

By default, the `background-image` property repeats an image both horizontally and vertically.

Some images should be repeated only horizontally or vertically, or they will look strange, like this:

```
body
{
   background-image:url('gradient2.png');
}
```

The result of this code is shown in Figure 4.5.

Try it yourself >>

```
<html>
<head>
<style type="text/css">
   body
   {
     background-image:url('gradient2.png');
   }
</style>
</head>

<body>
```

(continued)

(continued)

```
<h1>Hello World!</h1>
</body>

</html>
```

Figure 4.5

If the image is repeated only horizontally (**repeat-x**), the background will look better:

```
body
{
    background-image:url('gradient2.png');
    background-repeat:repeat-x;
}
```

The result of this code is shown in Figure 4.6.

Try it yourself >>

```
<html>
<head>
<style type="text/css">
    body
```

```
    {
      background-image:url('gradient2.png');
      background-repeat:repeat-x;
    }
</style>
</head>

<body>
<h1>Hello World!</h1>
</body>

</html>
```

Hello World!

Figure 4.6

Background Image—Set Position and No Repeat

Showing the image only once is specified by the background-repeat property:

> **TIP** When using a background image, use an image that does not disturb the text.

```
body
{
  background-image:url('img_tree.png');
  background-repeat:no-repeat;
}
```

The result of this code is shown in Figure 4.7.

```
<html>
<head>
<style type="text/css">
  body
  {
    background-image:url('img_tree.png');
    background-repeat:no-repeat;
  }
</style>
</head>

<body>
<h1>Hello World!</h1>
<p>Background image example.</p>
<p>The background image is only showing once, but it is
  disturbing the reader!</p>
</body>

</html>
```

Figure 4.7

In this example, the background image is shown in the same place as the text. We want to change the position of the image, so that it does not disturb the text too much.

The position of the image is specified by the `background-position` property:

```
body
{
  background-image:url('img_tree.png');
  background-repeat:no-repeat;
  background-position:top right;
}
```

The result of this code is shown in Figure 4.8.

Try it yourself >>

```
<html>
<head>

<style type="text/css">
  body
  {
    background-image:url('img_tree.png');
    background-repeat:no-repeat;
    background-position:top right;
    margin-right:200px;
  }
</style>

</head>

<body>
<h1>Hello World!</h1>
<p>Background no-repeat, set position example.</p>
<p>Now the background image is only shown once and
   positioned away from the text.</p>
<p>In this example we have also added a margin on the right
   side, so the background image will never disturb the
   text.</p>
</body>
</html>
```

Hello World!

Background no-repeat, set position example.

Now the background image is only shown once and positioned away from the text.

In this example we have also added a margin on the right side, so the background image will never disturb the text.

Figure 4.8

 For information about adding a margin to an element, see Chapter 13, "CSS Margin."

Background—Shorthand Property

As you can see from the previous examples, there are many properties to consider when dealing with backgrounds.

To shorten the code, it is also possible to specify all the properties in one single property. This is called a **shorthand property**.

The shorthand property for background is simply `background`:

```
body {background:#ffffff url('img_tree.png') no-repeat top
   right}
```

The result of this code is shown in Figure 4.9.

Try it yourself >>

```
<html>
<head>

<style type="text/css">
   body
```

```
    {
      background:#ffffff url('img_tree.png') no-repeat top
          right;
      margin-right:200px;
    }
  </style>

  </head>

  <body>
  <h1>Hello World!</h1>
  <p>Now the background image is only shown once and
      positioned away from the text.</p>
  <p>In this example we have also added a margin on the right
      side, so the background image will never disturb the
      text.</p>
  </body>

  </html>
```

Figure 4.9

When using the shorthand property, the order of the property values are:

1. background-color
2. background-image
3. background-repeat
4. background-attachment
5. background-position

It does not matter if one of the property values is missing, as long as the ones that are present are in the order shown in the list.

Set a Fixed Background Image

When the background image is fixed, it will not scroll with the rest of the page, as shown in Figure 4.10.

Try it yourself >>

```html
<html>
<head>
<style type="text/css">
  body
  {
    background-image:url('smiley.gif');
    background-repeat:no-repeat;
    background-attachment:fixed
  }
</style>
</head>

<body>
<p>The background-image is fixed. Try to scroll down the
   page.</p>
<p>The background-image is fixed. Try to scroll down the
   page.</p>
<p>The background-image is fixed. Try to scroll down the
   page.</p>
<p>The background-image is fixed. Try to scroll down the
   page.</p>
<p>The background-image is fixed. Try to scroll down the
   page.</p>
<p>The background-image is fixed. Try to scroll down the
   page.</p>
```

```
<p>The background-image is fixed. Try to scroll down the
   page.</p>
<p>The background-image is fixed. Try to scroll down the
   page.</p>
<p>The background-image is fixed. Try to scroll down the
   page.</p>
<p>The background-image is fixed. Try to scroll down the
   page.</p>
<p>The background-image is fixed. Try to scroll down the
   page.</p>
<p>The background-image is fixed. Try to scroll down the
   page.</p>
<p>The background-image is fixed. Try to scroll down the
   page.</p>
<p>The background-image is fixed. Try to scroll down the
   page.</p>
<p>The background-image is fixed. Try to scroll down the
   page.</p>
</body>
</html>
```

The background-image is fixed. Try to scroll down the page.

The background-image is fixed. Try to scroll down the page.

The background-image is fixed. Try to scroll down the page.

The background-image is fixed. Try to scroll down the page.

The background-image is fixed. Try to scroll down the page.

The background-image is fixed. Try to scroll down the page.

The background-image is fixed. Try to scroll down the page.

The background-image is fixed. Try to scroll down the page.

The background-image is fixed. Try to scroll down the page.

The background-image is fixed. Try to scroll down the page.

The background-image is fixed. Try to scroll down the page.

The background-image is fixed. Try to scroll down the page.

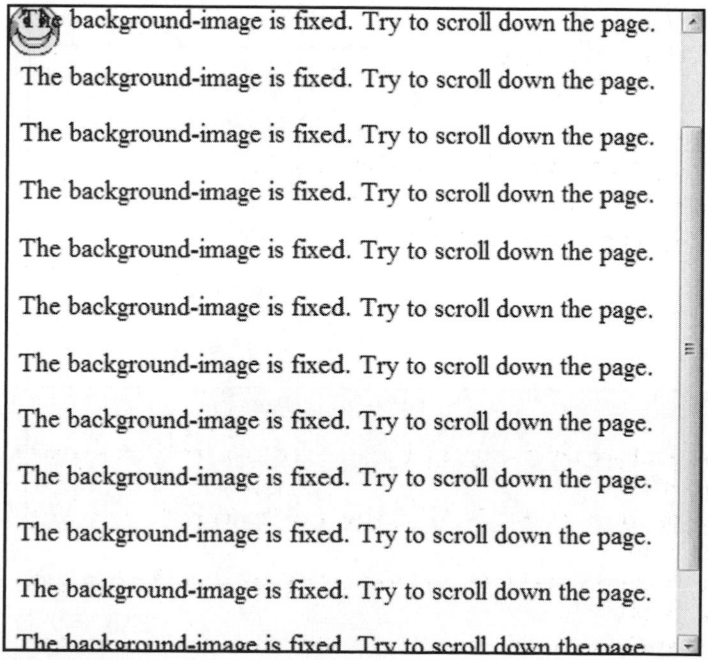

Figure 4.10

All CSS Background Properties

The number in the CSS column indicates in which CSS version the property is defined (CSS1 or CSS2).

Property	Description	Values	CSS
background	Sets all the background properties in one declaration	*background-color* *background-image* *background-repeat* *background-attachment* *background-position* inherit	1
background-attachment	Sets whether a background image is fixed or scrolls with the rest of the page	scroll fixed inherit	1
background-color	Sets the background color of an element	*color-rgb* *color-hex* *color-name* transparent inherit	1
background-image	Sets the background image for an element	url(*URL*) none inherit	1
background-position	Sets the starting position of a background image	top left top center top right center left center center center right bottom left bottom center bottom right *x% y%* *xpos ypos* inherit	1
background-repeat	Sets if/how a background image will be repeated	repeat repeat-x repeat-y no-repeat inherit	1

CHAPTER 5

STYLING TEXT

Text Formatting

This text is styled with some of the text formatting properties. The heading uses the text-align, text-transform, and color properties. The paragraph is indented, aligned, and the space between characters is specified. The underline is removed from the "Try it yourself" link.

Text Color

The color property is used to set the color of the text. The color can be specified by:

▸ Name—a color name, like red

▸ RGB—an RGB value, like rgb(255,0,0)

▸ Hex—a hex value, like #ff0000

The default color for a page is defined in the body selector.

```
body {color:blue}
h1 {color:#00ff00}
h2 {color:rgb(255,0,0)}
```

The result of this code is shown in Figure 5.1.

NOTE For W3C-compliant CSS: If you define the color property, you must also define the background-color property.

Try it yourself >>

```
<html>
<head>
<style type="text/css">
```

(continued)

39

(continued)

```
      body {color:red;}
      h1 {color:#00ff00;}
      p.ex {color:rgb(0,0,255);}
</style>
</head>

<body>
<h1>This is Heading 1</h1>
<p>This is an ordinary paragraph. Notice that this text is
    red. The default text-color for a page is defined in the
    body selector.</p>
<p class="ex">This is a paragraph with class="ex". This text
    is blue.</p>
</body>
</html>
```

> ## This is Heading 1
>
> This is an ordinary paragraph. Notice that this text is red. The default text-color for a page is defined in the body selector.
>
> This is a paragraph with class="ex". This text is blue.

Figure 5.1

Text Alignment

The text-align property is used to set the horizontal alignment of a text.

Text can be centered, aligned to the left or right, or justified.

When text-align is set to justify, each line is stretched so that every line has equal width, and the left and right margins are straight (like in magazines and newspapers).

```
h1 {text-align:center}
p.date {text-align:right}
p.main {text-align:justify}
```

The result of this code is shown in Figure 5.2.

40

Try it yourself >>

```
<html>
<head>
<style type="text/css">
  h1 {text-align:center;}
  p.date {text-align:right;}
  p.main {text-align:justify;}
</style>
</head>

<body>
<h1>CSS Text-Align Example</h1>
<p class="date">May 2009</p>
<p class="main">In my younger and more vulnerable years my
    father gave me some advice that I've been turning over in
    my mind ever since. "whenever you feel like criticizing
    anyone," he told me, "just remember that all the people in
    this world haven't had the advantages that you've had."
    </p>
<p><b>Note:</b> If you resize the browser window, the
    paragraph will adjust to stay justified.</p>
</body>

</html>
```

CSS Text-Align Example

May 2009

In my younger and more vulnerable years my father gave me some advice that I've been turning over in my mind ever since. "Whenever you feel like criticizing anyone," he told me, "just remember that all the people in this world haven't had the advantages that you've had."

Note: If you resize the browser window, the paragraph will adjust to stay justified.

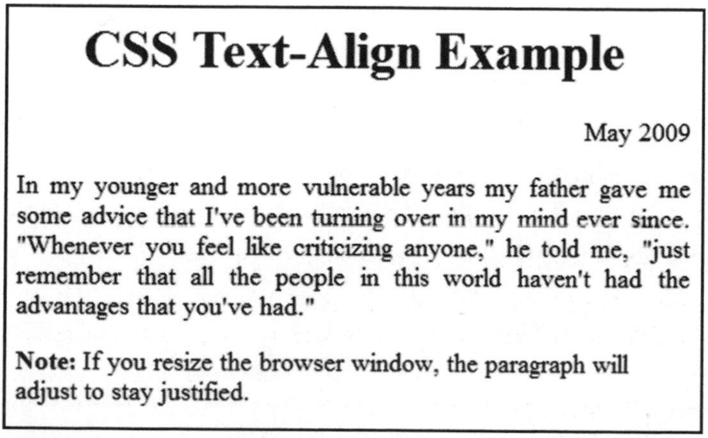

Figure 5.2

Text Decoration

The text-decoration property is used to set or remove decorations from text.

The text-decoration property is mostly used to remove underlines from links for design purposes:

```
a {text-decoration:none}
```

The result of this code is shown in Figure 5.3.

Try it yourself >>

```
<html>
<head>
<style type="text/css">
a {text-decoration:none;}
</style>
</head>

<body>
<p>Link to: <a href="http://www.w3schools.com">w3schools.
    com</a></p>
</body>

</html>
```

Link to: w3schools.com

Figure 5.3

It can also be used to decorate text:

```
h1 {text-decoration:overline}
h2 {text-decoration:line-through}
h3 {text-decoration:underline}
h4 {text-decoration:blink}
```

The result of this code is shown in Figure 5.4.

TIP Underlining text that is not a link often confuses users.

```html
<html>
<head>
<style type="text/css">
  h1 {text-decoration:overline;}
  h2 {text-decoration:line-through;}
  h3 {text-decoration:underline;}
  h4 {text-decoration:blink;}
</style>
</head>

<body>
<h1>This is Heading 1</h1>
<h2>This is Heading 2</h2>
<h3>This is Heading 3</h3>
<h4>This is Heading 4 (blinking)</h4>
<p><b>Note:</b> The "blink" value is not supported in IE,
  Chrome, or Safari.</p>
</body>

</html>
```

This is Heading 1

~~This is Heading 2~~

<u>This is Heading 3</u>

This is Heading 4 (blinking)

Note: The "blink" value is not supported in IE, Chrome, or Safari.

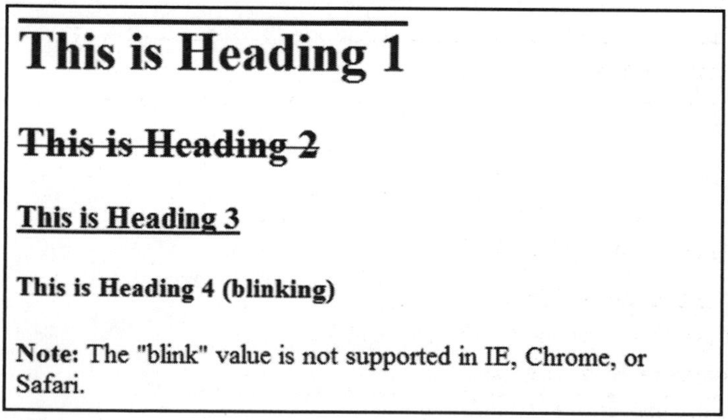

Figure 5.4

Text Transformation

The `text-transform` property is used to specify uppercase and lowercase letters in a text.

It can be used to turn everything into uppercase or lowercase letters or capitalize the first letter of each word.

```
p.uppercase {text-transform:uppercase}
p.lowercase {text-transform:lowercase}
p.capitalize {text-transform:capitalize}
```

The result of this code is shown in Figure 5.5.

Try it yourself >>

```
<html>
<head>
<style type="text/css">
  p.uppercase {text-transform:uppercase;}
  p.lowercase {text-transform:lowercase;}
  p.capitalize {text-transform:capitalize;}
</style>
</head>

<body>
<p class="uppercase">This is some text.</p>
<p class="lowercase">This is some text.</p>
<p class="capitalize">This is some text.</p>
</body>
</html>
```

THIS IS SOME TEXT.

this is some text.

This Is Some Text.

Figure 5.5

Text Indentation

The `text-indentation` property is used to specify the indentation of the first line of a text.

```
p {text-indent:50px}
```

The result of this code is shown in Figure 5.6.

Try it yourself >>

```
<html>
<head>
<style type="text/css">
  p {text-indent:50px;}
</style>
</head>
<body>


<p>In my younger and more vulnerable years my father gave me
   some advice that I've been turning over in my mind ever
   since. "whenever you feel like criticizing anyone," he
   told me, "Just remember that all the people in this world
   haven't had the advantages that you've had."</p>


</body>
</html>
```

> In my younger and more vulnerable years my father gave me some advice that I've been turning over in my mind ever since. "Whenever you feel like criticizing anyone," he told me, "just remember that all the people in this world haven't had the advantages that you've had."

Figure 5.6

More Properties

Here are some additional properties that you can use to format the text in your Web pages. For more information about each of these properties, see the Appendix, "CSS Reference."

Specify the Space between Characters

The `letter-spacing` property enables you to increase or decrease the space between characters, as shown in Figure 5.7.

```
<html>
<head>
<style type="text/css">
  h1 {letter-spacing:2px;}
  h2 {letter-spacing:-3px;}
</style>
</head>

<body>
<h1>This is Heading 1</h1>
<h2>This is Heading 2</h2>
</body>
</html>
```

This is Heading 1

This is Heading 2

Figure 5.7

Specify the Space between Lines

The `line-height` property enables you to specify the space between the lines in a paragraph, as shown in Figure 5.8.

```
<html>
<head>
<style type="text/css">
  p.small {line-height:90%;}
  p.big {line-height:200%;}
```

46

```
</style>
</head>

<body>
<p>
This is a paragraph with a standard line-height. The default
   line-height in most browsers is about 110% to 120%. This
   is a paragraph with a standard line-height.
</p>

<p class="small">
This is a paragraph with a smaller line-height. This is a
   paragraph with a smaller line-height. This is a paragraph
   with a smaller line-height.
</p>

<p class="big">
This is a paragraph with a bigger line-height. This is a
   paragraph with a bigger line-height. This is a paragraph
   with a bigger line-height.
</p>

</body>
</html>
```

This is a paragraph with a standard line-height. The default line-height in most browsers is about 110% to 120%. This is a paragraph with a standard line-height.

This is a paragraph with a smaller line-height. This is a paragraph with a smaller line-height. This is a paragraph with a smaller line-height.

This is a paragraph with a bigger line-height. This is a paragraph

with a bigger line-height. This is a paragraph with a bigger

line-height.

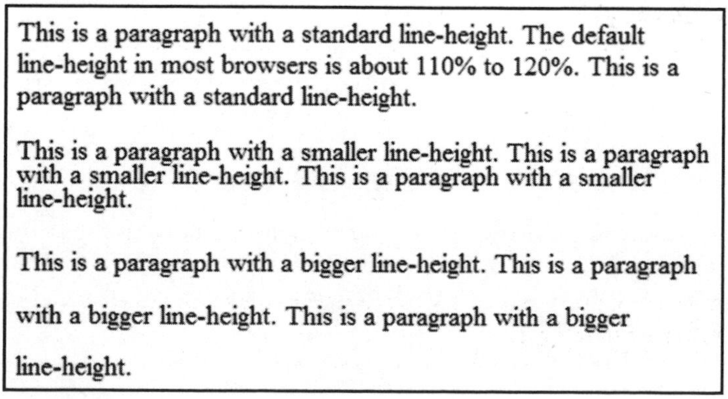

Figure 5.8

Set the Text Direction of an Element

The direction property enables you to change the text direction of an element. This is used primarily for displaying languages that are read from right to left. The result of this code is shown in Figure 5.9.

Try it yourself >>

```
<html>
<head>
<style type="text/css">
  div.ex1 {direction:rtl;}
</style>
</head>
<body>

<div>Some text. Default writing direction.</div>
<div class="ex1">Some text. Left-to-right direction.</div>

</body>
</html>
```

```
Some text. Default writing direction.
                        .Some text. Left-to-right direction
```

Figure 5.9

Increase the White Space Between Words

The word-spacing property enables you to increase the white space between words in a paragraph, as shown in Figure 5.10.

Try it yourself >>

```
<html>
<head>
<style type="text/css">
  p {word-spacing:30px;}
</style>
</head>
<body>
```

```
<p>
This is some text. This is some text.
</p>

</body>
</html>
```

This	is	some	text.	This	is	some
text.						

Figure 5.10

Disable Text Wrapping inside an Element

Using the nowrap value with the white-space property enables you to disable text wrapping inside an element, as shown in Figure 5.11.

Try it yourself >>

```
<html>
<head>
<style type="text/css">
  p {white-space:nowrap;}
</style>
</head>
<body>

<p>
This is some text. This is some text. This is some text.
   This is some text. This is some text. This is some text.
   This is some text. This is some text. This is some text.
   This is some text. This is some text. This is some text.
</p>

</body>
</html>
```

This is some text. This is some text. This is some text. This is som

Figure 5.11

Vertical Alignment of an Image

The `vertical-align` property enables you to set the vertical alignment of an image in text, as shown in Figure 5.12.

```
<html>
<head>
<style type="text/css">
  img.top {vertical-align:text-top;}
  img.super {vertical-align:super;}
</style>
</head>

<body>
<p>An image <img src="w3schools_logo.gif" alt="w3schools"
   width="270" height="50" />  inside a paragraph, with a
   default vertical alignment.</p>
<p> </p>
<p>An image <img class="top" src="w3schools_logo.gif"
   alt="w3schools" width="270" height="50" /> inside a
   paragraph, with a text-top alignment.</p>
<p> </p>
<p>An image <img class="super" src="w3schools_logo.gif"
   alt="w3schools" width="270" height="50" /> inside a
   paragraph, with a text-bottom alignment.</p>
</body>
</html>
```

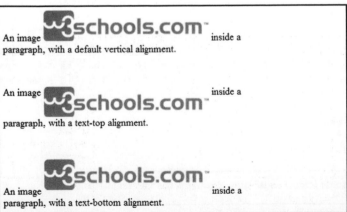

Figure 5.12

All CSS Text Properties

The number in the CSS column indicates in which CSS version the property is defined (CSS1 or CSS2).

Property	Description	Values	CSS
color	Sets the color of a text	*color*	1
direction	Sets the text direction	ltr rtl	2
line-height	Sets the distance between lines	normal *number* *length* %	1
letter-spacing	Increases or decreases the space between characters	normal *length*	1
text-align	Aligns the text in an element	left right center justify	1
text-decoration	Adds decoration to text	none underline overline line-through blink	1
text-indent	Indents the first line of text in an element	*length* %	1
text-shadow		none *color* *length*	
text-transform	Controls the letters in an element	none capitalize uppercase lowercase	1
unicode-bidi		normal embed bidi-override	2
vertical-align	Sets the vertical alignment of an element	baseline sub super top text-top middle bottom text-bottom *length* %	1
white-space	Sets how white space inside an element is handled	normal pre nowrap	1
word-spacing	Increases or decreases the space between words	normal *length*	1

CHAPTER 6

STYLING FONTS

CSS font properties define the font family, boldness, size, and the style of text.

Difference between Serif and Sans Serif Fonts

> **TIP** On computer screens, sans serif fonts are considered easier to read than serif fonts.

CSS Font Families

In CSS, there are two types of font family names:

▸▸ **Generic family**—A group of font families with a similar look (like "serif" or "monospace")

▸▸ **Font family**—A specific font family (like "Times New Roman" or "Arial")

Generic family	Font family	Description
Serif	Times New Roman Georgia	Serif fonts have small lines at the ends of some characters.
Sans serif	Arial Verdana	"Sans" means with-out—these fonts do not have the lines at the ends of characters.
Monospace	Courier New Lucida Console	All monospace char-acters have the same width.

Font Family

The font family of a text is set with the font-family property.

The font-family property should hold several font names as a "fallback" system. If the browser does not support the first font, it tries the next font.

Start with the font you want and end with a generic family to let the browser pick a similar font in the generic family if no other fonts are available. Figure 6.1 shows two different fonts on a page.

NOTE If the name of a font family is more than one word, it must be in quotation marks, like font-family:"Times New Roman".

More than one font family is specified in a comma-separated list:

```
p{font-family:"Times New Roman", Times, serif}
```

Try it yourself >>

```
<html>
<head>
<style type="text/css">
  p.serif{font-family:"Times New Roman",Times,serif;}
  p.sansserif{font-family:Arial,Helvetica,sans-serif;}
</style>
</head>

<body>
<h1>CSS Font-Family</h1>
<p class="serif">This is a paragraph shown in the Times New
  Roman font.</p>
```

(continued)

(continued)

```
<p class="sansserif">This is a paragraph shown in the Arial
   font.</p>

</body>
</html>
```

CSS Font-Family

This is a paragraph shown in the Times New Roman font.

This is a paragraph shown in the Arial font.

Figure 6.1

For a list of commonly used font combinations, see the Appendix, "Web Safe Font Combinations."

Font Style

The `font-style` property is mostly used to specify italic text, as shown in Figure 6.2.

This property has three values:

▸▸ **Normal**—The text is shown normally.

▸▸ **Italic**—The text is shown in italics.

▸▸ **Oblique**—The text is "leaning" (oblique is very similar to italic, but less supported).

```
p.normal {font-style:normal}
p.italic {font-style:italic}
p.oblique {font-style:oblique}
```

Try it yourself >>

```
<html>
<head>
<style type="text/css">
   p.normal {font-style:normal;}
   p.italic {font-style:italic;}
```

```
    p.oblique {font-style:oblique;}
</style>
</head>

<body>
<p class="normal">This is a paragraph, normal.</p>
<p class="italic">This is a paragraph, italic.</p>
<p class="oblique">This is a paragraph, oblique.</p>
</body>

</html>
```

This is a paragraph, normal.

This is a paragraph, italic.

This is a paragraph, oblique.

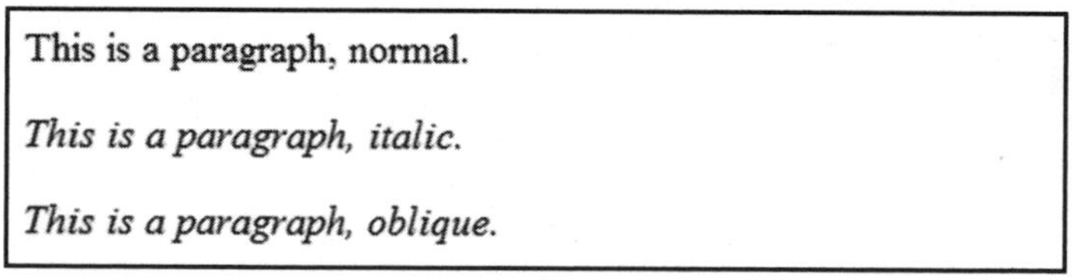

Figure 6.2

Font Size

The `font-size` property sets the size of the text.

Being able to manage the text size is important in Web design. However, you should not use font size adjustments to make paragraphs look like headings or headings look like paragraphs.

Always use the proper HTML tags, like <h1> – <h6> for headings and <p> for paragraphs.

The `font-size` value can be an absolute or relative size.

Absolute size

▸▸ Sets the text to a specified size

▸▸ Does not allow a user to change the text size in all browsers (bad for accessibility reasons)

▸▸ Is useful when the physical size of the output is known

Relative size

▸▸ Sets the size relative to surrounding elements

▸▸ Allows a user to change the text size in browsers

> **N O T E** If you do not specify a font size, the default size for normal text, like paragraphs, is 16px (16px=1em).

Set Font Size with Pixels

Setting the text size with pixels gives you full control over the text size. Figure 6.3 shows the result of this code:

```
h1 {font-size:40px}
h2 {font-size:30px}
p {font-size:14px}
```

Try it yourself >>

```
<html>
<head>
<style>
  h1 {font-size:40px;}
  h2 {font-size:30px;}
  p {font-size:14px;}
</style>
</head>
<body>

<h1>This is Heading 1</h1>
<h2>This is Heading 2</h2>
<p>This is a paragraph.</p>
<p>Specifying the font-size in px allows Firefox, Chrome,
   and Safari to resize the text, but not Internet
   Explorer.</p>

</body>
</html>
```

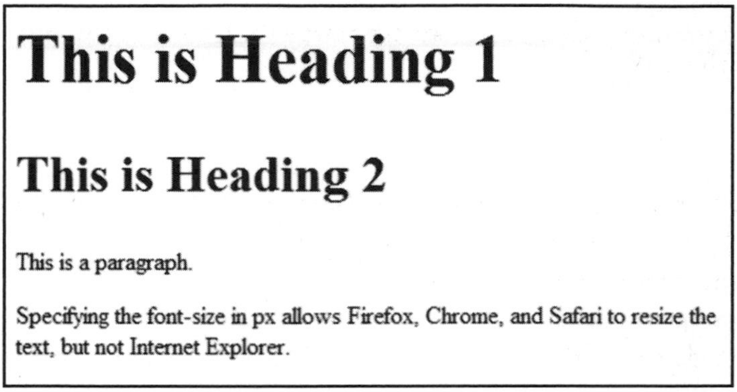

This is Heading 1

This is Heading 2

This is a paragraph.

Specifying the font-size in px allows Firefox, Chrome, and Safari to resize the text, but not Internet Explorer.

Figure 6.3

This example allows Firefox, Chrome, and Safari to resize the text, *but not Internet Explorer*.

The text can be resized in all browsers using the Zoom tool (however, this resizes the entire page, not just the text).

Set Font Size with Em

To avoid the resizing problem with Internet Explorer, many developers use em size units instead of pixels.

The em size unit is recommended by the World Wide Web Consortium (W3C).

1em is equal to the current font size. The default text size in browsers is 16px, so the default size of 1em is 16px.

The size can be calculated from pixels to em using this formula: *pixels/16=em.* Figure 6.4 shows the result of this code:

```
h1 {font-size:2.5em} /* 40px/16=2.5em */
h2 {font-size:1.875em} /* 30px/16=1.875em */
p {font-size:0.875em} /* 14px/16=0.875em */
```

Try it yourself >>

```
<html>
<head>
<style>
  h1 {font-size:2.5em;} /* 40px/16=2.5em */
  h2 {font-size:1.875em;} /* 30px/16=1.875em */
```

(continued)

(continued)

```
    p {font-size:0.875em;} /* 14px/16=0.875em */
</style>
</head>
<body>

<h1>This is Heading 1</h1>
<h2>This is Heading 2</h2>
<p>This is a paragraph.</p>
<p>Specifying the font-size in em allows Internet Explorer,
    Firefox, Chrome, and Safari to resize the text.
    Unfortunately, there is still a problem with IE. When
    resizing the text, it becomes larger/smaller than it
    should.
</p>
</body>
</html>
```

This is Heading 1

This is Heading 2

This is a paragraph.

Specifying the font-size in em allows Internet Explorer, Firefox, Chrome, and Safari to resize the text. Unfortunately, there is still a problem with IE. When resizing the text, it becomes larger/smaller than it should.

Figure 6.4

In this example, the text size in em is the same as the previous example in pixels. However, with the em size, it is possible to adjust the text size in all browsers.

Unfortunately, there is still a problem with IE. When resizing the text, it becomes larger than it should when made larger, and smaller than it should when made smaller.

Use a Combination of Percent and Em

The solution that works in all browsers is to set a default font-size in percent for the body element. Figure 6.5 shows the result of this code:

```
body {font-size:100%}
h1 {font-size:2.5em}
h2 {font-size:1.875em}
p {font-size:0.875em}
```

```
<html>
<head>
<style>
  body {font-size:100%;}
  h1 {font-size:2.5em;}
  h2 {font-size:1.875em;}
  p {font-size:0.875em;}
</style>
</head>
<body>

<h1>This is Heading 1</h1>
<h2>This is Heading 2</h2>
<p>This is a paragraph.</p>
<p>Specifying the font-size in percent and em displays the
   same size in all browsers, and allows all browsers to
   resize the text!</p>

</body>
</html>
```

This is Heading 1

This is Heading 2

This is a paragraph.

Specifying the font-size in percent and em displays the same size in all browsers, and allows all browsers to resize the text!

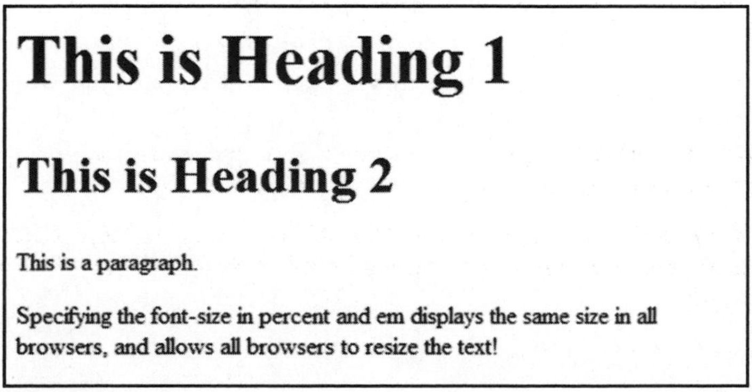

Figure 6.5

Our code now works great! It shows the same text size in all browsers and allows all browsers to zoom or resize the text!

More Properties

Here are some additional properties that you can use to format the fonts in your Web pages. For more information about each of these properties, see the Appendix, "CSS Reference."

Set the Boldness of the Font

The `font-weight` property enables you to set the boldness of a font. Figure 6.6 shows the result of this code:

Try it yourself >>

```
<html>
<head>
<style type="text/css">
  p.normal {font-weight:normal;}
  p.light {font-weight:lighter;}
  p.thick {font-weight:bold;}
  p.thicker {font-weight:900;}
</style>
</head>

<body>
<p class="normal">This is a normal paragraph.</p>
<p class="light">This is a light paragraph.</p>
<p class="thick">This is a bold paragraph.</p>
<p class="thicker">This is a paragraph with a weight of
   900.</p>
</body>

</html>
```

This is a normal paragraph.

This is a light paragraph.

This is a bold paragraph.

This is a paragraph with a weight of 900.

Figure 6.6

Set the Variant of the Font

The `font-variant` property enables you to set the variant of a font. Figure 6.7 shows the result of this code:

Try it yourself >>

```
<html>
<head>
<style type="text/css">
  p.normal {font-variant:normal;}
  p.small {font-variant:small-caps;}
</style>
</head>

<body>
<p class="normal">This paragraph is in a normal font.</p>
<p class="small">This paragraph is in small caps.</p>
</body>

</html>
```

This paragraph is in a normal font.

THIS PARAGRAPH IS IN SMALL CAPS.

Figure 6.7

All the Font Properties in One Declaration

This example demonstrates how to use the shorthand property for setting all of the font properties in one declaration. Figure 6.8 shows the result of this code:

Try it yourself >>

```
<html>
<head>
<style type="text/css">
  p.ex1 {font:15px arial,sans-serif;}
  p.ex2 {font:italic bold 12px/30px Georgia,serif;}
</style>
</head>

<body>
<p class="ex1">This is a paragraph. This is a paragraph.
  This is a paragraph. This is a paragraph. This is a
  paragraph. This is a paragraph. This is a paragraph. This
  is a paragraph.</p>
<p class="ex2">This is a paragraph. This is a paragraph.
  This is a paragraph. This is a paragraph. This is a
  paragraph. This is a paragraph. This is a paragraph. This
  is a paragraph.</p>
</body>
</html>
```

> This is a paragraph. This is a paragraph. This is a paragraph.
> This is a paragraph. This is a paragraph. This is a paragraph.
> This is a paragraph. This is a paragraph.
>
> *This is a paragraph. This is a paragraph. This is a paragraph.*
>
> *This is a paragraph. This is a paragraph. This is a paragraph.*
>
> *This is a paragraph. This is a paragraph.*

Figure 6.8

All CSS Font Properties

The number in the CSS column indicates in which CSS version the property is defined (CSS1 or CSS2).

Property	Description	Values	CSS
font	Sets all the font properties in one declaration	*font-style* *font-variant* *font-weight* *font-size/line-height* *font-family* caption icon menu message-box small-caption status-bar inherit	1
font-family	Specifies the font family for text	*family-name* *generic-family* inherit	1
font-size	Specifies the font size of text	xx-small x-small small medium large x-large xx-large smaller larger *length* % inherit	1
font-style	Specifies the font style for text	normal italic oblique inherit	1
font-variant	Specifies whether or not a text should be displayed in a small-caps font	normal small-caps inherit	1
font-weight	Specifies the weight of a font	normal bold bolder lighter 100 200 300 400 500 600 700 800 900 inherit	1

CHAPTER 7

STYLING LINKS

Links can be styled in different ways.

Styling Links

Links can be styled with any CSS property (for example, `color`, `font-family`, `background-color`).

Links are special because they can be styled differently depending on what state they are in.

The four links states are

▶ `a:link`—A normal, unvisited link

▶ `a:visited`—A link the user has visited

▶ `a:hover`—A link when the user mouses over it

▶ `a:active`—A link the moment it is clicked

```
a:link {color:#FF0000}      /* unvisited link */
a:visited {color:#00FF00}   /* visited link */
a:hover {color:#FF00FF}     /* mouse over link */
a:active {color:#0000FF}    /* selected link */
```

Figure 7.1 has been modified to show all the states of the links for this property.

Try it yourself >>

```
<html>
<head>
<style type="text/css">
  a:link {color:#FF0000;}    /* unvisited link */
  a:visited {color:#00FF00;} /* visited link */
  a:hover {color:#FF00FF;}   /* mouse over link */
  a:active {color:#0000FF;}  /* selected link */
```

```
</style>
</head>

<body>
<p><b><a href="default.asp" target="_blank">This is a link
    </a></b></p>
<p>This link is red when the page is opened.</p>
<p><b><a href="default.asp" target="_blank">This is a link
    </a></b></p>
<p>It turns purple when the mouse moves over it,</p>
<p><b><a href="default.asp" target="_blank">This is a link
    </a></b></p>
<p>blue when the mouse clicks on it, </p>
<p><b><a href="default.asp" target="_blank">This is a link
    </a></b></p>
<p>and green to show that the link has been visited.</p>
</body>
</html>
```

This is a link

This link is red when the page is opened.

This is a link

It turns purple when the mouse moves over it,

This is a link

blue when the mouse clicks on it,

This is a link

and green to show that the link has been visited.

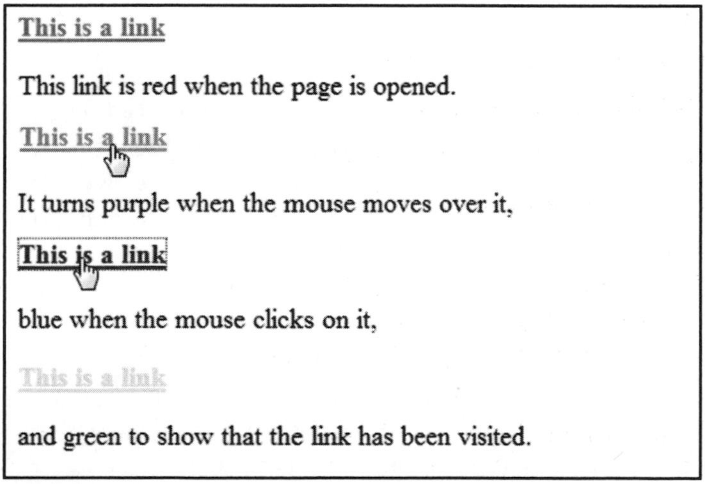

Figure 7.1

N O T E When setting the style for several link states, there are some order rules:

▸▸   a:hover must come after a:link and a:visited
▸▸   a:active must come after a:hover

Common Link Styles

In the previous example the link changes color depending on what state it is in.

Let's go through some of the other common ways to style links.

Text Decoration

The text-decoration property is mostly used to remove underlines from links.

```
a:link {text-decoration:none}
a:visited {text-decoration:none}
a:hover {text-decoration:underline}
a:active {text-decoration:underline}
```

Figure 7.2 has been modified to show all the states of the links for this property.

> **Try it yourself >>**

```
<html>
<head>
<style type="text/css">
  a:link {text-decoration:none;}      /* unvisited link */
  a:visited {text-decoration:none;}   /* visited link */
  a:hover {text-decoration:underline;} /* mouse over link */
  a:active {text-decoration:underline;} /* selected link */
</style>
</head>

<body>
<p><b><a href="default.asp" target="_blank">This is a link
  </a></b></p>
<p>This link does not have an underline </p>
<p><b><a href="default.asp" target="_blank">This is a link
  </a></b></p>
<p>except on mouseover </p>
<p><b><a href="default.asp" target="_blank">This is a link
  </a></b></p>
<p>and during the click.</p>
</body>
</html>
```

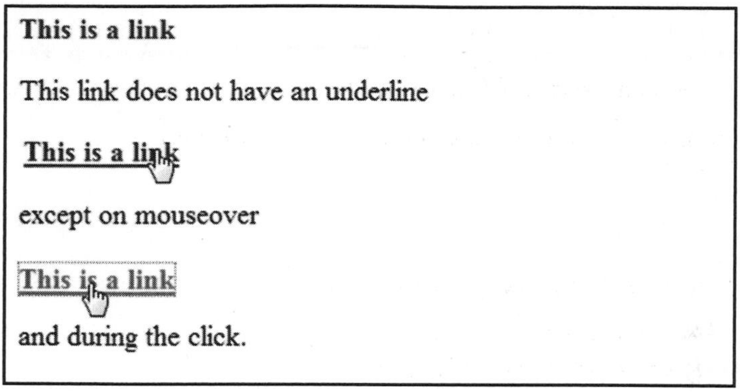

This is a link

This link does not have an underline

This is a link

except on mouseover

This is a link

and during the click.

Figure 7.2

Background Color

The background-color property specifies the background color for links:

```
a:link {background-color:#B2FF99;}
a:visited {background-color:#FFFF85;}
a:hover {background-color:#FF704D;}
a:active {background-color:#FF704D;}
```

Figure 7.3 has been modified to show all the states of the links for this property.

Try it yourself >>

```
<html>
<head>
<style type="text/css">
  a:link {background-color:#B2FF99;} /* unvisited link */
  a:visited {background-color:#FFFF85;} /* visited link */
  a:hover {background-color:#FF704D;} /* mouse over link */
  a:active {background-color:#FF704D;} /* selected link */
</style>
</head>

<body>
<p><b><a href="default.asp" target="_blank">This is a link
  </a></b></p>
```

(continued)

67

(continued)

```
<p>This link is blue with a light green background before it
   is clicked,</p>
<p><b><a href="default.asp" target="_blank">This is a link
   </a></b></p>
<p>blue with an orange background on mouseover,</p>
<p><b><a href="default.asp" target="_blank">This is a link
   </a></b></p>
<p> red with an orange background on mouseclick,</p>
<p><b><a href="default.asp" target="_blank">This is a link
   </a></b></p>
<p>and blue with a yellow background after the click.</p>
</body>
</html>
```

<u>**This is a link**</u>

This link is blue with a light green background before it is clicked,

blue with an orange background on mouseover,

red with an orange background on mouseclick,

<u>**This is a link**</u>

and blue with a yellow background after the click.

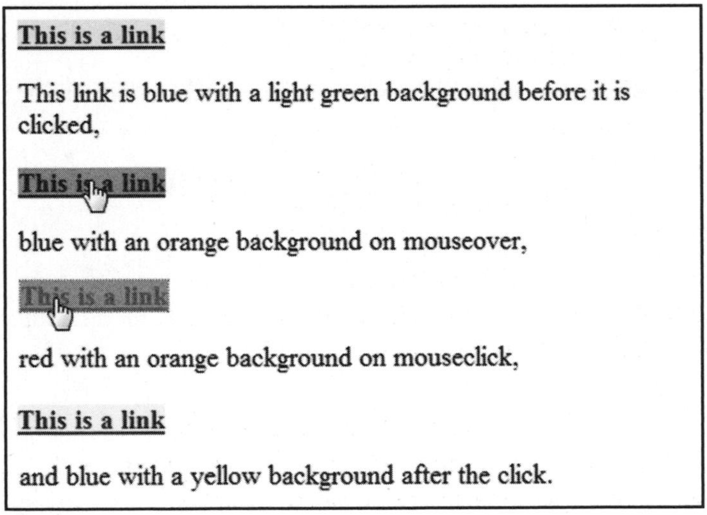

Figure 7.3

More Properties

Here are some additional properties that you can use to format the links in your Web pages.

For more information about each of these properties, see the CSS Reference pages on the w3schools Web site.

Add Different Styles to Hyperlinks

This example demonstrates how to add other styles to hyperlinks. Figure 7.4 has been modified to show all the states of the links for these properties.

```
<html>
<head>
<style type="text/css">
  a.one:link {color:#ff0000;}
  a.one:visited {color:#0000ff;}
  a.one:hover {color:#ffcc00;}

  a.two:link {color:#ff0000;}
  a.two:visited {color:#0000ff;}
  a.two:hover {font-size:150%;}

  a.three:link {color:#ff0000;}
  a.three:visited {color:#0000ff;}
  a.three:hover {background:#66ff66;}

  a.four:link {color:#ff0000;}
  a.four:visited {color:#0000ff;}
  a.four:hover {font-family:monospace;}

  a.five:link {color:#ff0000;text-decoration:none;}
  a.five:visited {color:#0000ff;text-decoration:none;}
  a.five:hover {text-decoration:underline;}
</style>
</head>

<body>
<p>Mouse over the links to see them change layout.</p>

<p><b><a class="one" href="default.asp" target=
  "_blank">This link changes color</a></b></p>
<p><b><a class="two" href="default.asp" target=
  "_blank">This link changes font-size</a></b></p>
<p><b><a class="three" href="default.asp" target=
  "_blank">This link changes background-color</a></b></p>
```

(continued)

(continued)

```
<p><b><a class="four" href="default.asp" target="_blank">This
   link changes font-family</a></b></p>
<p><b><a class="five" href="default.asp" target="_blank">This
   link changes text-decoration</a></b></p>
</body>
</html>
```

Mouse over the links to see them change layout.

This link changes color

This link changes color

This link changes font-size

This link changes font-size

This link changes background-color

This link changes background-color

This link changes font-family

`This link changes font-family`

This link changes text-decoration

This link changes text-decoration

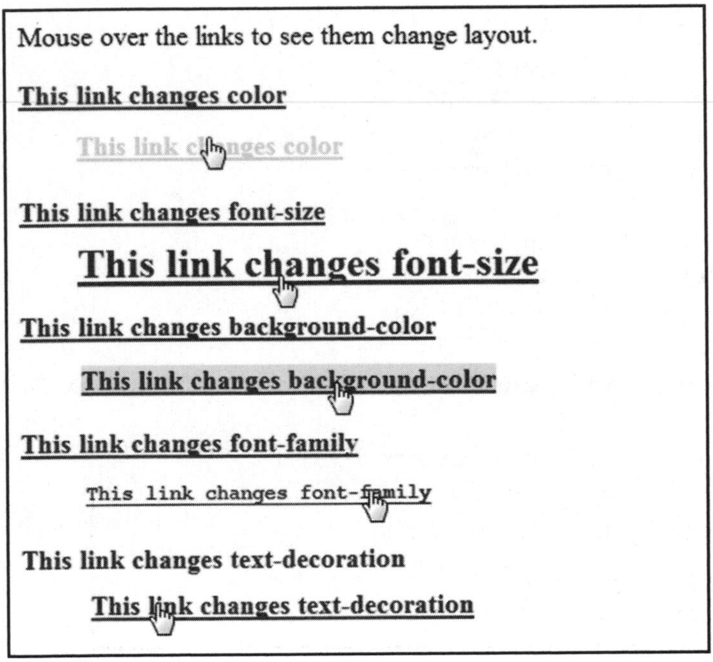

Figure 7.4

Advanced—Create Link Boxes

This example demonstrates a more advanced example where we combine several CSS properties to display links as boxes. Figure 7.5 has been modified to show all the states of the links for this property.

Try it yourself >>

```
<html>
<head>
<style type="text/css">
   a:link,a:visited
   {
```

70

```
    display:block;
    font-weight:bold;
    color:#FFFFFF;
    background-color:#98bf21;
    width:120px;
    text-align:center;
    padding:4px;
    text-decoration:none;
  }
  a:hover,a:active
  {
    background-color:#7A991A;
  }
</style>
</head>

<body>
<a href="default.asp" target="_blank">This is a link</a>
</body>
</html>
```

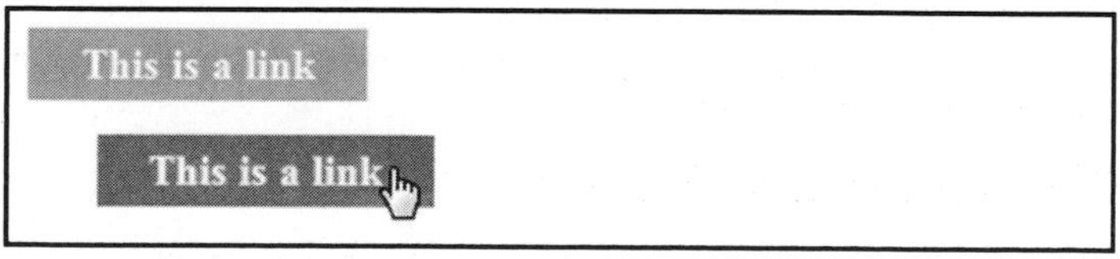

Figure 7.5

71

CHAPTER 8

STYLING LISTS

The CSS list properties allow you to

- ❑ Set different list item markers for ordered lists
- ❑ Set different list item markers for unordered lists
- ❑ Set an image as the list item marker

List

In HTML, there are two types of lists:

▸▸ **Unordered lists**—The list items are marked with bullets.

▸▸ **Ordered lists**—The list items are marked with numbers or letters.

With CSS, lists can be styled further, and images can be used as the list item marker.

Different List Item Markers

The type of list item marker is specified with the `list-style-type` property:

```
ul.a {list-style-type: circle;}
ul.b {list-style-type: square;}

ol.c {list-style-type: upper-roman;}
ol.d {list-style-type: lower-alpha;}
```

Figure 8.1 shows the results of this code.

Try it yourself >>

```
<html>
<head>
<style type="text/css">
  ul.a {list-style-type:circle;}
```

```
  ul.b {list-style-type:square;}
  ol.c {list-style-type:upper-roman;}
  ol.d {list-style-type:lower-alpha;}
</style>
</head>

<body>
<p>Example of unordered lists:</p>

<ul class="a">
  <li>Coffee</li>
  <li>Tea</li>
  <li>Coca Cola</li>
</ul>

<ul class="b">
  <li>Coffee</li>
  <li>Tea</li>
  <li>Coca Cola</li>
</ul>

<p>Example of ordered lists:</p>

<ol class="c">
  <li>Coffee</li>
  <li>Tea</li>
  <li>Coca Cola</li>
</ol>

<ol class="d">
  <li>Coffee</li>
  <li>Tea</li>
  <li>Coca Cola</li>
</ol>

</body>
</html>
```

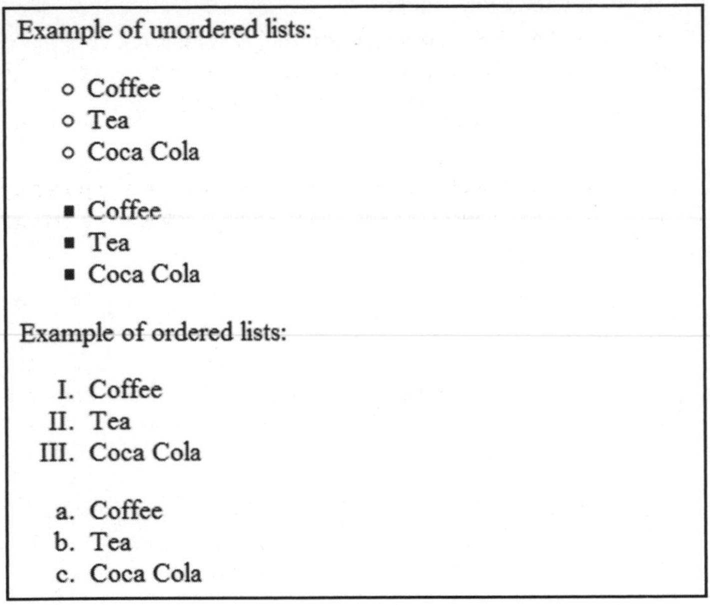

Example of unordered lists:

- ○ Coffee
- ○ Tea
- ○ Coca Cola

- ■ Coffee
- ■ Tea
- ■ Coca Cola

Example of ordered lists:

  I. Coffee
 II. Tea
III. Coca Cola

  a. Coffee
  b. Tea
  c. Coca Cola

Figure 8.1

Some of the property values are for unordered lists, and some for ordered lists.

Values for Unordered Lists

Value	Description
none	No marker.
disc	Default. The marker is a filled circle.
circle	The marker is a circle.
square	The marker is a square.

Values for Ordered Lists

Value	Description
armenian	The marker is traditional Armenian numbering.
decimal	The marker is a number.
decimal-leading-zero	The marker is a number padded by initial zeros (01, 02, 03, etc.).
georgian	The marker is traditional Georgian numbering (an, ban, gan, etc.).
lower-alpha	The marker is lower-alpha (a, b, c, d, e, etc.).
lower-greek	The marker is lower-greek (alpha, beta, gamma, etc.).
lower-latin	The marker is lower-latin (a, b, c, d, e, etc.).
lower-roman	The marker is lower-roman (i, ii, iii, iv, v, etc.).

Value	Description
upper-alpha	The marker is upper-alpha (A, B, C, D, E, etc.).
upper-latin	The marker is upper-latin (A, B, C, D, E, etc.).
upper-roman	The marker is upper-roman (I, II, III, IV, V, etc.).

NOTE No versions of Internet Explorer (including IE8) support the property values `decimal-leading-zero`, `lower-greek`, `lower-latin`, `upper-latin`, `armenian`, or `georgian`.

An Image as the List Item Marker

To specify an image as the list item marker, use the `list-style-image` property:

```
ul
{
  list-style-image: url('sqpurple.gif');
}
```

This example does not display equally in all browsers. IE and Opera will display the image-marker a little bit higher than Firefox, Chrome, and Safari.

If you want the image-marker to be placed equally in all browsers, a cross-browser solution is explained in the next section.

Figure 8.2 shows the results of this code.

Try it yourself >>

```
<html>
<head>
<style type="text/css">
  ul
  {
    list-style-image:url('sqpurple.gif');
  }
</style>
</head>

<body>
<ul>
  <li>Coffee</li>
```

(continued)

75

(continued)

```
    <li>Tea</li>
    <li>Coca Cola</li>
  </ul>
  </body>
  </html>
```

■ Coffee
■ Tea
■ Coca Cola

Figure 8.2

Cross-Browser Solution

The following example displays the image-marker equally in all browsers:

```
ul
  {
    list-style-type: none;
    padding: 0px;
    margin: 0px;
  }
li
  {
    background-image: url(sqpurple.gif);
    background-repeat: no-repeat;
    background-position: 0px 5px;
    padding-left: 14px;
  }
```

Example explained:

▸▸ For ul

- Set the list-style-type to none to remove the list item marker.

- Set both padding and margin to 0px (for cross-browser compatibility).

▸▸ For li

- Set the URL of the image and show it only once (no-repeat).

- Position the image where you want it (left 0px and down 5px).

- Position the text in the list with padding-left.

Figure 8.3 shows the results of this code.

Try it yourself >>

```
<html>
<head>
<style type="text/css">
  ul
  {
    list-style-type:none;
    padding:0px;
    margin:0px;
  }
  li
  {
    background-image:url(sqpurple.gif);
    background-repeat:no-repeat;
    background-position:0px 5px;
    padding-left:14px;
  }
</style>
</head>

<body>
<ul>
  <li>Coffee</li>
  <li>Tea</li>
  <li>Coca Cola</li>
</ul>
</body>

</html>
```

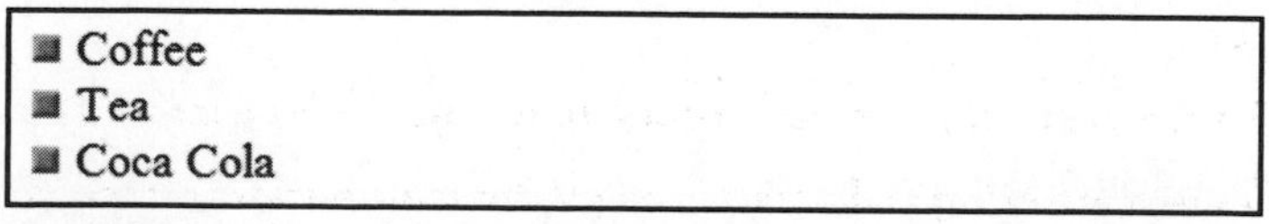

■ Coffee
■ Tea
■ Coca Cola

Figure 8.3

Shorthand Property

It is also possible to specify all the list properties in one, single property. This is called a *shorthand property*.

The shorthand property used for lists is the `list-style` property:

```
ul
{
  list-style: square url("sqpurple.gif");
}
```

When using the shorthand property, the order of the values is

1. `list-style-type`
2. `list-style-position` (for a description, see the CSS Properties table at the end of the chapter)
3. `list-style-image`

It does not matter if one of the preceding values is missing as long as the rest are in the specified order.

Figure 8.4 shows the results of this code.

Try it yourself >>

```
<html>
<head>
<style type="text/css">
  ul
  {
    list-style:square url("sqpurple.gif");
  }
</style>
</head>

<body>
<ul>
  <li>Coffee</li>
  <li>Tea</li>
  <li>Coca Cola</li>
</ul>
</body>
</html>
```

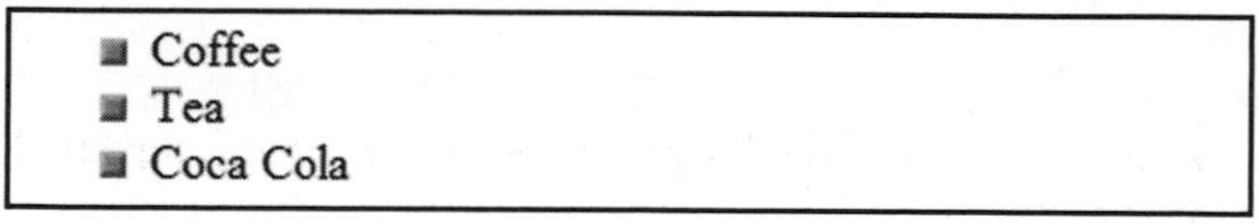

- Coffee
- Tea
- Coca Cola

Figure 8.4

All the Different List-Item Markers for Lists

This example demonstrates all the different list-item markers in CSS. Because this example is so long, we have laid part of the code out in columns and modified Figure 8.5 to show all the results of the code on one page.

Try it yourself >>

```
<html>
<head>
<style type="text/css">
  ul.a {list-style-type:disc;}
  ul.b {list-style-type:circle;}
  ul.c {list-style-type:square;}
  ul.d {list-style-type:none;}
  ol.e {list-style-type:decimal;}
  ol.f {list-style-type:decimal-leading-zero;}
  ol.g {list-style-type:lower-roman;}
  ol.h {list-style-type:upper-roman;}
  ol.i {list-style-type:lower-alpha;}
  ol.j {list-style-type:upper-alpha;}
  ol.k {list-style-type:lower-greek;}
  ol.l {list-style-type:lower-latin;}
  ol.m {list-style-type:upper-latin;}
  ol.n {list-style-type:armenian;}
  ol.o {list-style-type:georgian;}
</style>
</head>
```

(continued)

(continued)

```
<body>
<ul class="a">
  <li>Disc type</li>
  <li>Tea</li>
  <li>Coca Cola</li>
</ul>

<ul class="b">
  <li>Circle type</li>
  <li>Tea</li>
  <li>Coca Cola</li>
</ul>

<ul class="c">
  <li>Square type</li>
  <li>Tea</li>
  <li>Coca Cola</li>
</ul>

<ul class="d">
  <li>The "none" type</li>
  <li>Tea</li>
  <li>Coca Cola</li>
</ul>

<ol class="e">
  <li>Decimal type</li>
  <li>Tea</li>
  <li>Coca Cola</li>
</ol>

<ol class="f">
  <li>Decimal-leading-zero
  type</li>
  <li>Tea</li>
  <li>Coca Cola</li>
</ol>

<ol class="g">
  <li>Lower-roman type
    </li>
```

```
  <li>Tea</li>
  <li>Coca Cola</li>
</ol>

<ol class="h">
  <li>Upper-roman type
    </li>
  <li>Tea</li>
  <li>Coca Cola</li>
</ol>

<ol class="i">
  <li>Lower-alpha type
    </li>
  <li>Tea</li>
  <li>Coca Cola</li>
</ol>

<ol class="j">
  <li>Upper-alpha type
    </li>
  <li>Tea</li>
  <li>Coca Cola</li>
</ol>

<ol class="k">
  <li>Lower-greek type
    </li>
  <li>Tea</li>
  <li>Coca Cola</li>
</ol>

<ol class="l">
  <li>Lower-latin type
    </li>
  <li>Tea</li>
  <li>Coca Cola</li>
</ol>

<ol class="m">
  <li>Upper-latin type
    </li>
```

```
    <li>Tea</li>                           <ol class="o">
    <li>Coca Cola</li>                       <li>Georgian type</li>
</ol>                                        <li>Tea</li>
                                             <li>Coca Cola</li>
<ol class="n">                           </ol>
  <li>Armenian type</li>
  <li>Tea</li>                           </body>
  <li>Coca Cola</li>                     </html>
</ol>
```

- Disc type
- Tea
- Coca Cola

○ Circle type
○ Tea
○ Coca Cola

■ Square type
■ Tea
■ Coca Cola

  The "none" type
  Tea
  Coca Cola

1. Decimal type
2. Tea
3. Coca Cola

01. Decimal-leading-zero type
02. Tea
03. Coca Cola

i. Lower-roman type
ii. Tea
iii. Coca Cola

I. Upper-roman type
II. Tea
III. Coca Cola

a. Lower-alpha type
b. Tea
c. Coca Cola

A. Upper-alpha type
B. Tea
C. Coca Cola

α. Lower-greek type
β. Tea
γ. Coca Cola

a. Lower-latin type
b. Tea
c. Coca Cola

A. Upper-latin type
B. Tea
C. Coca Cola

Ա. Armenian type
Բ. Tea
Գ. Coca Cola

ა. Georgian type
ბ. Tea
გ. Coca Cola

Figure 8.5 This list has been laid out in two columns for space considerations, but in a browser the page would display in one long column.

All CSS List Properties

The number in the CSS column indicates in which CSS version the property is defined (CSS1 or CSS2).

Property	Description	Values	CSS
list-style	Sets all the properties for a list in one declaration	*list-style-type* *list-style-position* *list-style-image* inherit	1
list-style-image	Specifies an image as the list-item marker	URL*(url)* none inherit	1
list-style-position	Specifies if the list-item markers should appear inside or outside the content flow	inside outside inherit	1
list-style-type	Specifies the type of list-item marker	none disc circle square decimal decimal-leading-zero armenian georgian lower-alpha upper-alpha lower-greek lower-latin upper-latin lower-roman upper-roman inherit	1

CHAPTER 9

STYLING TABLES

The look of an HTML table can be greatly improved with CSS:

Company	Contact	Country
Alfreds Futterkiste	Maria Anders	Germany
Berglunds Snabbköp	Christina Berglund	Sweden
Centro Comercial Moctezuma	Francisco Chang	Mexico
Ernst Handel	Roland Mendel	Austria
Island Trading	Helen Bennett	UK
Königlich Essen	Philip Cramer	Germany
Laughing Bacchus Winecellars	Yoshi Tannamuri	Canada
Magazzini Alimentari Riuniti	Giovanni Rovelli	Italy
North/South	Simon Crowther	UK
Paris Spécialités	Marie Bertrand	France
The Big Cheese	Liz Nixon	USA
Vaffeljernet	Palle Ibsen	Denmark

Table Borders

To specify table borders in CSS, use the border property.

The following example specifies a black border for `table`, `th`, and `td` elements:

```
table, th, td
{
   border: 1px solid black;
}
```

Figure 9.1 shows the results of this code.

```
<html>
<head>
<style type="text/css">
  table, th, td
  {
    border:1px solid black;
  }
</style>
</head>

<body>
<table>
  <tr>
    <th>Firstname</th>
    <th>Lastname</th>
  </tr>
  <tr>
    <td>Peter</td>
    <td>Griffin</td>
  </tr>
  <tr>
    <td>Lois</td>
    <td>Griffin</td>
  </tr>
</table>
</body>
</html>
```

Firstname	Lastname
Peter	Griffin
Lois	Griffin

Figure 9.1

Notice that the table in this example has double borders. This is because the `table`, `th`, and `td` elements each have separate borders.

To display a single border for the table, use the `border-collapse` property.

Collapse Borders

The `border-collapse` property sets whether the table borders are collapsed into a single border or separated:

```
table
{
  border-collapse:collapse;
}
table, th, td
{
  border: 1px solid black;
}
```

Figure 9.2 shows the results of this code.

Try it yourself >>

```
<!DOCTYPE html PUBLIC "-//W3C//DTD XHTML 1.0 Transitional//
  EN" "http://www.w3.org/TR/xhtml1/DTD/xhtml1-transitional.
  dtd">
<html>
<head>
<style type="text/css">
  table
  {
    border-collapse:collapse;
  }
  table, td, th
  {
    border:1px solid black;
  }
</style>
</head>

<body>
<table>
  <tr>
    <th>Firstname</th>
    <th>Lastname</th>
  </tr>
```

(continued)

85

(continued)

```
    <tr>
      <td>Peter</td>
      <td>Griffin</td>
    </tr>
    <tr>
      <td>Lois</td>
      <td>Griffin</td>
    </tr>
  </table>
  <p><b>Note:</b> If a !DOCTYPE is not specified, the border-
    collapse property can produce unexpected results.</p>
  </body>
  </html>
```

Firstname	Lastname
Peter	Griffin
Lois	Griffin

Note: If a !DOCTYPE is not specified, the border-collapse property can produce unexpected results.

Figure 9.2

Table Width and Height

Width and height of a table is defined by the width and height properties.

This example sets the width of the table to 100%, and the height of the th elements to 50px:

```
table
{
  width:100%;
}
th
{
  height:50px;
}
```

Figure 9.3 shows the results of this code.

```html
<html>
<head>
<style type="text/css">
  table, td, th
  {
    border:1px solid black;
  }
  table
  {
    width:100%;
  }
  th
  {
    height:50px;
  }
</style>
</head>

<body>
<table>
  <tr>
    <th>Firstname</th>
    <th>Lastname</th>
    <th class="savings">Savings</th>
  </tr>
  <tr>
    <td>Peter</td>
    <td>Griffin</td>
    <td>$100</td>
  </tr>
  <tr>
    <td>Lois</td>
    <td>Griffin</td>
    <td>$150</td>
  </tr>
  <tr>
    <td>Joe</td>
    <td>Swanson</td>
```

(continued)

(continued)

```
        <td>$300</td>
     </tr>
     <tr>
        <td>Cleveland</td>
        <td>Brown</td>
        <td>$250</td>
     </tr>
  </table>
  </body>
  </html>
```

Firstname	Lastname	Savings
Peter	Griffin	$100
Lois	Griffin	$150
Joe	Swanson	$300
Cleveland	Brown	$250

Figure 9.3

Table Text Alignment

The text in a table is aligned with the text-align and vertical-align properties.

The text-align property sets the horizontal alignment, like left, right, or center:

```
td
{
   text-align:right;
}
```

Figure 9.4 shows the results of this code.

Try it yourself >>

```
<html>
<head>
```

```
<style type="text/css">
  table, td, th
  {
    border:1px solid black;
  }
  td
  {
    text-align:right;
  }
</style>
</head>

<body>
<table>
  <tr>
    <th>Firstname</th>
    <th>Lastname</th>
    <th>Savings</th>
  </tr>
  <tr>
    <td>Peter</td>
    <td>Griffin</td>
    <td>$100</td>
  </tr>
  <tr>
    <td>Lois</td>
    <td>Griffin</td>
    <td>$150</td>
  </tr>
  <tr>
    <td>Joe</td>
    <td>Swanson</td>
    <td>$300</td>
  </tr>
  <tr>
    <td>Cleveland</td>
    <td>Brown</td>
    <td>$250</td>
  </tr>
</table>
```

(continued)

(continued)
```
  </body>
  </html>
```

Firstname	Lastname	Savings
Peter	Griffin	$100
Lois	Griffin	$150
Joe	Swanson	$300
Cleveland	Brown	$250

Figure 9.4

The `vertical-align` property sets the vertical alignment, like `top`, `bottom`, or `middle`:

```
td
{
  height:50px;
  vertical-align:bottom;
}
```

Figure 9.5 shows the results of this code.

Try it yourself >>

```
<html>
<head>
<style type="text/css">
  table, td, th
  {
    border:1px solid black;
  }
  td
  {
    height:50px;
    vertical-align:bottom;
  }
```

```
    </style>
    </head>

    <body>
    <table>
      <tr>
        <th>Firstname</th>
        <th>Lastname</th>
        <th>Savings</th>
      </tr>
      <tr>
        <td>Peter</td>
        <td>Griffin</td>
        <td>$100</td>
      </tr>
      <tr>
        <td>Lois</td>
        <td>Griffin</td>
        <td>$150</td>
      </tr>
      <tr>
        <td>Joe</td>
        <td>Swanson</td>
        <td>$300</td>
      </tr>
      <tr>
        <td>Cleveland</td>
        <td>Brown</td>
        <td>$250</td>
      </tr>
    </table>
    </body>
    </html>
```

Firstname	Lastname	Savings
Peter	Griffin	$100
Lois	Griffin	$150
Joe	Swanson	$300
Cleveland	Brown	$250

Figure 9.5

Table Padding

To control the space between the border and content in a table, use the padding property on td and th elements:

```
td
{
  padding:15px;
}
```

Figure 9.6 shows the results of this code.

Try it yourself >>

```
<html>
<head>
<style type="text/css">
  table, td, th
  {
    border:1px solid black;
  }
  td
  {
```

```
        padding:15px;
    }
</style>
</head>

<body>
<table>
  <tr>
    <th>Firstname</th>
    <th>Lastname</th>
    <th>Savings</th>
  </tr>
  <tr>
    <td>Peter</td>
    <td>Griffin</td>
    <td>$100</td>
  </tr>
  <tr>
    <td>Lois</td>
    <td>Griffin</td>
    <td>$150</td>
  </tr>
  <tr>
    <td>Joe</td>
    <td>Swanson</td>
    <td>$300</td>
  </tr>
  <tr>
    <td>Cleveland</td>
    <td>Brown</td>
    <td>$250</td>
  </tr>
</table>
</body>
</html>
```

Firstname	Lastname	Savings
Peter	Griffin	$100
Lois	Griffin	$150
Joe	Swanson	$300
Cleveland	Brown	$250

Figure 9.6

Table Color

The following example specifies the color of the borders, and the text and background color of th elements:

```
table, td, th
{
  border:1px solid green;
}
th
{
  background-color:green;
  color:white;
}
```

Figure 9.7 shows the results of this code.

Try it yourself >>

```
<html>
<head>
<style type="text/css">
  table, td, th
  {
```

```
    border:1px solid green;
  }
  th
  {
    background-color:green;
    color:white;
  }
</style>
</head>

<body>
<table>
  <tr>
    <th>Firstname</th>
    <th>Lastname</th>
    <th>Savings</th>
  </tr>
  <tr>
    <td>Peter</td>
    <td>Griffin</td>
    <td>$100</td>
  </tr>
  <tr>
    <td>Lois</td>
    <td>Griffin</td>
    <td>$150</td>
  </tr>
  <tr>
    <td>Joe</td>
    <td>Swanson</td>
    <td>$300</td>
  </tr>
  <tr>
    <td>Cleveland</td>
    <td>Brown</td>
    <td>$250</td>
  </tr>
</table>
</body>
</html>
```

Firstname	Lastname	Savings
Peter	Griffin	$100
Lois	Griffin	$150
Joe	Swanson	$300
Cleveland	Brown	$250

Figure 9.7

More Properties

Here are some additional properties that you can use to format the tables in your Web pages.

For more information about each of these properties, see the Appendix, "CSS Reference."

Make a Fancy Table

This example demonstrates how to use a variety of the table properties to create a fancy table.

Figure 9.8 shows the results of this code.

Try it yourself >>

```
<html>
<head>
<style type="text/css">
  #customers
  {
    font-family:"Trebuchet MS", Arial, Helvetica, sans-
  serif;
    width:100%;
    border-collapse:collapse;
  }
  #customers td, #customers th
  {
    font-size:1em;
    border:1px solid #98bf21;
```

```
    padding:3px 7px 2px 7px;
  }
  #customers th
  {
    font-size:1.1em;
    text-align:left;
    padding-top:5px;
    padding-bottom:4px;
    background-color:#A7C942;
    color:#ffffff;
  }
  #customers tr.alt td
  {
    color:#000000;
    background-color:#EAF2D3;
  }
</style>
</head>

<body>
<table id="customers">
  <tr>
    <th>Company</th>
    <th>Contact</th>
    <th>Country</th>
  </tr>
  <tr>
    <td>Alfreds Futterkiste</td>
    <td>Maria Anders</td>
    <td>Germany</td>
  </tr>
  <tr class="alt">
    <td>Berglunds Snabbköp</td>
    <td>Christina Berglund</td>
    <td>Sweden</td>
  </tr>
  <tr>
    <td>Centro Comercial Moctezuma</td>
    <td>Francisco Chang</td>
    <td>Mexico</td>
```

(continued)

97

(continued)

```
      </tr>
      <tr class="alt">
        <td>Ernst Handel</td>
        <td>Roland Mendel</td>
        <td>Austria</td>
      </tr>
      <tr>
        <td>Island Trading</td>
        <td>Helen Bennett</td>
        <td>UK</td>
      </tr>
      <tr class="alt">
        <td>Königlich Essen</td>
        <td>Philip Cramer</td>
        <td>Germany</td>
      </tr>
      <tr>
        <td>Laughing Bacchus Winecellars</td>
        <td>Yoshi Tannamuri</td>
        <td>Canada</td>
      </tr>
      <tr class="alt">
        <td>Magazzini Alimentari Riuniti</td>
        <td>Giovanni Rovelli</td>
        <td>Italy</td>
      </tr>
      <tr>
        <td>North/South</td>
        <td>Simon Crowther</td>
        <td>UK</td>
      </tr>
      <tr class="alt">
        <td>Paris Spécialités</td>
        <td>Marie Bertrand</td>
        <td>France</td>
      </tr>
    </table>
    </body>
    </html>
```

Company	Contact	Country
Alfreds Futterkiste	Maria Anders	Germany
Berglunds Snabbköp	Christina Berglund	Sweden
Centro Comercial Moctezuma	Francisco Chang	Mexico
Ernst Handel	Roland Mendel	Austria
Island Trading	Helen Bennett	UK
Königlich Essen	Philip Cramer	Germany
Laughing Bacchus Winecellars	Yoshi Tannamuri	Canada
Magazzini Alimentari Riuniti	Giovanni Rovelli	Italy
North/South	Simon Crowther	UK
Paris Spécialités	Marie Bertrand	France

Figure 9.8

Set the Position of the Table Caption

This example demonstrates how to use the caption property to position the table caption.

Try it yourself >>

```
<!DOCTYPE html PUBLIC "-//W3C//DTD XHTML 1.0 Transitional//
  EN" "http://www.w3.org/TR/xhtml1/DTD/xhtml1-transitional.
  dtd">
<html>
<head>
<style type="text/css">
  caption {caption-side:bottom;}
</style>
</head>

<body>

<table border="1">
```

(continued)

(continued)

```
<caption>Table 1.1 Customers</caption>
  <tr>
    <th>Company</th>
    <th>Contact</th>
    <th>Country</th>
  </tr>
  <tr>
    <td>Alfreds Futterkiste</td>
    <td>Maria Anders</td>
    <td>Germany</td>
  </tr>
  <tr>
    <td>Berglunds Snabbköp</td>
    <td>Christina Berglund</td>
    <td>Sweden</td>
  </tr>
  <tr>
    <td>Centro Comercial Moctezuma</td>
    <td>Francisco Chang</td>
    <td>Mexico</td>
  </tr>
  <tr>
    <td>Ernst Handel</td>
    <td>Roland Mendel</td>
    <td>Austria</td>
  </tr>
  <tr>
    <td>Island Trading</td>
    <td>Helen Bennett</td>
    <td>UK</td>
  </tr>
  <tr>
    <td>Magazzini Alimentari Riuniti</td>
    <td>Giovanni Rovelli</td>
    <td>Italy</td>
  </tr>
  <tr>
    <td>North/South</td>
    <td>Simon Crowther</td>
    <td>UK</td>
```

```
    </tr>
</table>

<p><b>Note:</b> Internet Explorer 8 (and higher) supports
   the caption-side property if a !DOCTYPE is specified.</p>
</body>
</html>
```

Company	Contact	Country
Alfreds Futterkiste	Maria Anders	Germany
Berglunds Snabbköp	Christina Berglund	Sweden
Centro Comercial Moctezuma	Francisco Chang	Mexico
Ernst Handel	Roland Mendel	Austria
Island Trading	Helen Bennett	UK
Magazzini Alimentari Riuniti	Giovanni Rovelli	Italy
North/South	Simon Crowther	UK

Table 1.1 Customers

Note: Internet Explorer 8 (and higher) supports the caption-side property if a !DOCTYPE is specified.

Figure 9.9

Section III
CSS Box Model

CHAPTER 10

CSS BOX MODEL

All HTML elements can be considered as boxes. In CSS, the term **box model** is used when talking about design and layout.

The CSS box model is essentially a box that wraps around HTML elements, and it consists of margins, borders, padding, and the actual content.

The box model allows us to place a border around elements and space elements in relation to other elements.

The following image illustrates the box model:

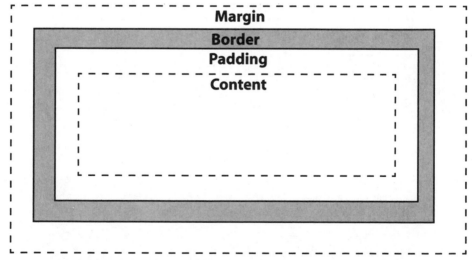

Explanation of the different parts:

▸▸ **Margin**—Clears an area around the border. The margin does not have a background color, and it is completely transparent.

▸▸ **Border**—A border that lies around the padding and content. The border is affected by the background color of the box.

▸▸ **Padding**—Clears an area around the content. The padding is affected by the background color of the box.

▸▸ **Content**—The content of the box, where text and images appear.

In order to set the width and height of an element correctly in all browsers, you need to know how the box model works.

Width and Height of an Element

The total width of the element in the following example is 300px:

```
width:250px;
padding:10px;
border:5px solid gray;
margin:10px;
```

N O T E When you specify the width and height properties of an element with CSS, you are just setting the width and height of the content area. To know the full size of the element, you must also add the padding, border, and margin.

Let's do the math:

250px (width)

+ 20px (10px left + 10px right padding)

+ 10px (5px left + 5px right border)

+ 20px (10px left + 10px right margin)

= 300px

Imagine that you only had 250px of space. Let's make an element with a total width of 250px:

```
width:220px;
padding:10px;
border:5px solid gray;
margin:0px;
```

Figure 10.1 shows the result of this code.

Try it yourself >>

```
<html>
<head>
```

```
<style type="text/css">
  div.ex
  {
    width:220px;
    padding:10px;
    border:5px solid gray;
    margin:0px;
  }
</style>
</head>

<body>
<img src="250px.gif" width="250" height="1" /><br /><br />

<div class="ex">The line above is 250px wide.<br />
The total width of this element is also 250px.</div>

</body>
</html>
```

The line above is 250px wide.
The total width of this element is
also 250px.

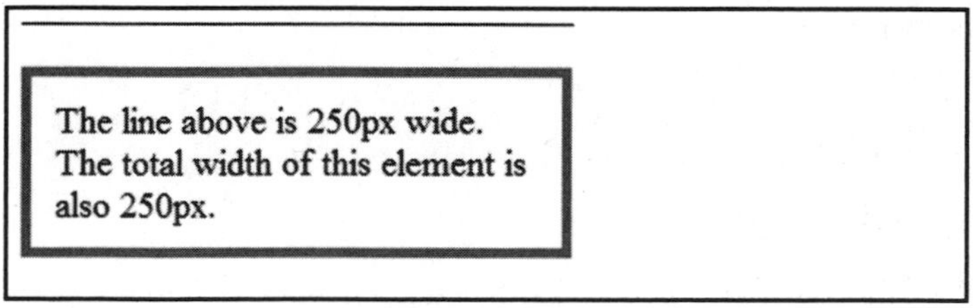

Figure 10.1

NOTE This example will not display correctly in IE! However, we will solve that problem in the next example.

The **total width** of an element should always be calculated like this:

Total element width = width + left padding + right padding + left border + right border + left margin + right margin

The **total height** of an element should always be calculated like this:

Total element height = height + top padding + bottom padding + top border + bottom border + top margin + bottom margin

Browser Compatibility Issue

If you tested the previous example in Internet Explorer, you saw that the total width was not exactly 250px.

IE includes padding and border in the width, when the width property is set, **unless a !DOCTYPE is declared.**

To fix this problem, just add a !DOCTYPE to the code:

```
<!DOCTYPE html PUBLIC "-//W3C//DTD XHTML 1.0 Transitional//
  EN"
"http://www.w3.org/TR/xhtml1/DTD/xhtml1-transitional.dtd">
<html>
<head>
<style type="text/css">
  div.ex
  {
    width:220px;
    padding:10px;
    border:5px solid gray;
    margin:0px;
  }
</style>
</head>
```

Figure 10.2 shows the result of this code.

Try it yourself >>

```
<!DOCTYPE html PUBLIC "-//W3C//DTD XHTML 1.0 Transitional//
  EN" "http://www.w3.org/TR/xhtml1/DTD/xhtml1-transitional.
  dtd">
<html>
<head>
<style type="text/css">
  div.ex
  {
    width:220px;
    padding:10px;
    border:5px solid gray;
```

```
    margin:0px;
  }
  </style>
</head>

<body>
<img src="250px.gif" width="250" height="1" /><br /><br />

<div class="ex">The line above is 250px wide.<br />
Now the total width of this element is also 250px.</div>

<p><b>Note:</b> In this example we have added a !DOCTYPE
    declaration (above the html element), so it displays
    correctly in all browsers.</p>

</body>
</html>
```

The line above is 250px wide.
Now the total width of this
element is also 250px.

Note: In this example we have added a DOCTYPE declaration
(above the html element), so it displays correctly in all browsers.

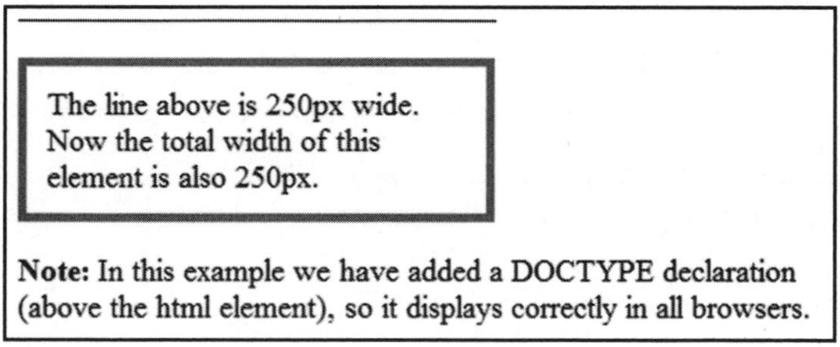

Figure 10.2

CHAPTER 11

CSS BORDER

CSS Border Properties

The CSS border properties allow you to specify the style and color of an element's border.

Border Style

The `border-style` property specifies what kind of border to display.

NOTE None of the other border properties will have any effect unless `border-style` is set.

Border-Style Values

none: Defines no border

dotted: Defines a dotted border

dashed: Defines a dashed border

solid: Defines a solid border

double: Defines two borders. The width of the two borders are the same as the border-width value

groove: Defines a 3D grooved border. The effect depends on the border-color value

ridge: Defines a 3D ridged border. The effect depends on the border-color value

inset: Defines a 3D inset border. The effect depends on the border-color value

outset: Defines a 3D outset border. The effect depends on the border-color value

Try it yourself >>

```
<html>
<head>
<style type="text/css">
  p.none {border-style:none;}
  p.dotted {border-style:dotted;}
  p.dashed {border-style:dashed;}
  p.solid {border-style:solid;}
  p.double {border-style:double;}
  p.groove {border-style:groove;}
  p.ridge {border-style:ridge;}
  p.inset {border-style:inset;}
  p.outset {border-style:outset;}
  p.hidden {border-style:hidden;}
</style>
</head>

<body>
<p class="none">No border.</p>
<p class="dotted">A dotted border.</p>
<p class="dashed">A dashed border.</p>
<p class="solid">A solid border.</p>
<p class="double">A double border.</p>
<p class="groove">A groove border.</p>
<p class="ridge">A ridge border.</p>
<p class="inset">An inset border.</p>
<p class="outset">An outset border.</p>
<p class="hidden">A hidden border.</p>
</body>

</html>
```

Figure 11.1 shows the result of this code.

| No border. |
| A dotted border. |
| A dashed border. |
| A solid border. |
| A double border. |
| A groove border. |
| A ridge border. |
| An inset border. |
| An outset border. |
| A hidden border. |

Figure 11.1

TIP Border styles will look slightly different in different browsers. For example, in Internet Explorer the dots in a dotted border are diamonds, while they are actual circles in Firefox and squares in Chrome. The inset and outset borders will also come out differently depending on the browser, but the effect will be similar.

Border Width

The border-width property is used to set the width of the border.

The width is set in pixels or by using one of the three predefined values: thin, medium, or thick.

NOTE The border-width property does not work if it is used alone. Use the border-style property to set the borders first.

```
p.one
{
  border-style:solid;
  border-width:5px;
}
p.two
{
  border-style:solid;
  border-width:medium;
}
```

Figure 11.2 shows the result of this code.

Try it yourself >>

```
<html>
<head>
<style type="text/css">
  p.one
  {
    border-style:solid;
    border-width:5px;
  }
  p.two
  {
    border-style:solid;
    border-width:medium;
  }
  p.three
  {
    border-style:solid;
    border-width:1px;
  }
</style>
</head>

<body>
<p class="one">Some text.</p>
<p class="two">Some text.</p>
<p class="three">Some text.</p>
```

(continued)

113

(continued)

```
<p><b>Note:</b> The "border-width" property does not work if
   it is used alone. Use the "border-style" property to set
   the borders first.</p>
</body>

</html
```

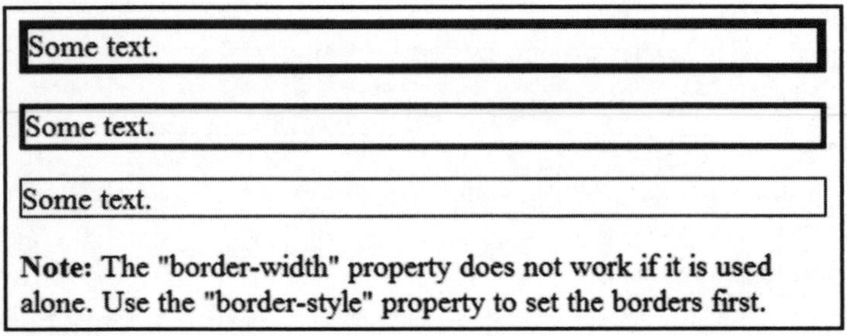

Some text.

Some text.

Some text.

Note: The "border-width" property does not work if it is used alone. Use the "border-style" property to set the borders first.

Figure 11.2

Border Color

The border-color property is used to set the color of the border. The color can be set by:

▸ **Name**—Specify a color name, like red

▸ **RGB**—Specify an RGB value, like rgb(255,0,0)

▸ **Hex**—Specify a hex value, like #ff0000

You can also set the border color to transparent.

NOTE The border-color property does not work if it is used alone. Use the border-style property to set the borders first.

```
p.one
{
  border-style:solid;
  border-color:red;
}
p.two
{
  border-style:solid;
```

```
    border-color:#98bf21;
  }
```

Figure 11.3 shows the result of this code.

```
<html>
<head>
<style type="text/css">
  p.one
  {
    border-style:solid;
    border-color:red;
  }
  p.two
  {
    border-style:solid;
    border-color:#98bf21;
  }
</style>
</head>

<body>
<p class="one">A solid red border</p>
<p class="two">A solid green border</p>
<p><b>Note:</b> The "border-color" property does not work if
  it is used alone. Use the "border-style" property to set
  the borders first.</p>
</body>
</html>
```

A solid red border

A solid green border

Note: The "border-color" property does not work if it is used alone. Use the "border-style" property to set the borders first.

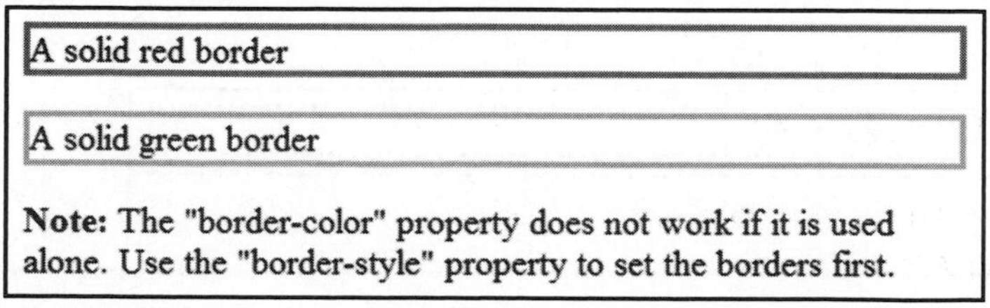

Figure 11.3

Border—Individual Sides

In CSS, it is possible to specify different borders for different sides:

```
p
{
    border-top-style:dotted;
    border-right-style:solid;
    border-bottom-style:dotted;
    border-left-style:solid;
}
```

Figure 11.4 shows the result of this code.

Try it yourself >>

```
<html>
<head>
<style type="text/css">
    p
    {
        border-top-style:dotted;
        border-right-style:solid;
        border-bottom-style:dotted;
        border-left-style:solid;
    }
</style>
</head>

<body>
<p>2 different border styles.</p>
</body>
</html>
```

2 different border styles.

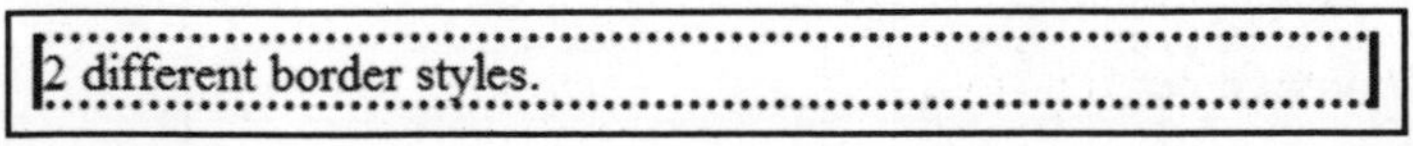

Figure 11.4

The previous example can also be set with a single property:

```
border-style:dotted solid;
```

Figure 11.5 shows the result of this code.

```
<html>
<head>
<style type="text/css">
  p
  {
    border-style:dotted solid;
  }
</style>
</head>

<body>
<p>2 different border styles.</p>
</body>
</html>
```

2 different border styles.

Figure 11.5

The `border-style` property can have from one to four values.

▸▸ `border-style:dotted solid double dashed;`

- Top border is dotted.

- Right border is solid.

- Bottom border is double.

- Left border is dashed.

▸▸ `border-style:dotted solid double;`

- Top border is dotted.

- Right and left borders are solid.

- Bottom border is double.

▸▸ `border-style:dotted solid;`

- Top and bottom borders are dotted.

- Right and left borders are solid.

‣ `border-style:dotted;`

- All four borders are dotted.

The `border-style` property is used in the previous example. However, it also works with `border-width` and `border-color`.

Border—Shorthand Property

As you can see from the previous examples, there are many properties to consider when dealing with borders.

To shorten the code, it is also possible to specify all the border properties in one property. This is called a **shorthand property.**

The shorthand property for the border properties is `border`:

```
border:5px solid red;
```

Figure 11.6 shows the result of this code.

Try it yourself >>

```
<html>
<head>
<style type="text/css">
  p
  {
    border:5px solid red;
  }
</style>
</head>

<body>
<p>This is some text in a paragraph.</p>
</body>
</html>
```

This is some text in a paragraph.

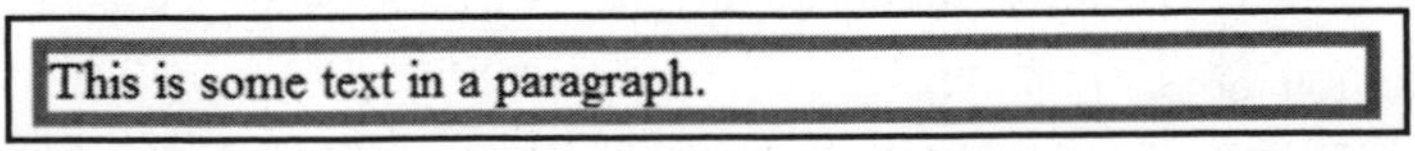

Figure 11.6

When using the border property, the order of the values is

▸▸ `border-width`

▸▸ `border-style`

▸▸ `border-color`

It does not matter if one of the preceding values is missing (although `border-style` is required), as long as the rest are in the specified order.

 See the CSS Border chapter on the w3schools Web site, www.w3schools. com/css/css_border.asp, for more examples of ways to combine CSS commands to create additional border styles.

All CSS Border Properties

The number in the CSS column indicates in which CSS version the property is defined (CSS1 or CSS2).

Property	Description	Values	CSS
border	Sets all the border properties in one declaration	*border-width* *border-style* *border-color*	1
border-bottom	Sets all the bottom border properties in one declaration	*border-bottom-width* *border-bottom-style* *border-bottom-color*	1
border-bottom-color	Sets the color of the bottom border	*border-color*	2
border-bottom-style	Sets the style of the bottom border	*border-style*	2
border-bottom-width	Sets the width of the bottom border	*border-width*	1
border-color	Sets the color of the four borders	*color_name* *hex_number* *rgb_number* transparent inherit	1
border-left	Sets all the left border properties in one declaration	*border-left-width* *border-left-style* *border-left-color*	1
border-left-color	Sets the color of the left border	*border-color*	2
border-left-style	Sets the style of the left border	*border-style*	2

(continued)

Property	Description	Values	CSS
border-left-width	Sets the width of the left border	*border-width*	1
border-right	Sets all the right border properties in one declaration	*border-right-width border-right-style border-right-color*	1
border-right-color	Sets the color of the right border	*border-color*	2
border-right-style	Sets the style of the right border	*border-style*	2
border-right-width	Sets the width of the right border	*border-width*	1
border-style	Sets the style of the four borders	none hidden dotted dashed solid double groove ridge inset outset inherit	1
border-top	Sets all the top border properties in one declaration	*border-top-width border-top-style border-top-color*	1
border-top-color	Sets the color of the top border	*border-color*	2
border-top-style	Sets the style of the top border	*border-style*	2
border-top-width	Sets the width of the top border	*border-width*	1
border-width	Sets the width of the four borders	thin medium thick *length* inherit	1

CHAPTER 12

CSS OUTLINES

An outline is a line that is drawn around elements, outside the border edge, to make the element stand out.

The outline properties specify the style, color, and width of an outline.

> **NOTE** Internet Explorer 8 (and higher) supports the outline properties if a !DOCTYPE is specified.

Outline

Use the outline property to draw a line around an element, outside the border edge.

Try it yourself >>

```
<!DOCTYPE html PUBLIC "-//W3C//DTD XHTML 1.0 Transitional//
   EN" "http://www.w3.org/TR/xhtml1/DTD/xhtml1-transitional.
   dtd">
<html>
<head>
<style type="text/css">
  p
  {
    border:1px solid;
    outline:green dotted thick;
  }
</style>
</head>

<body>
<p><b>Note:</b> Internet Explorer 8 (and higher) supports
   the outline property
```

(continued)

121

(continued)

```
        if a !DOCTYPE is specified.</p>
    </body>
    </html>
```

Figure 12.1 shows the result of this code.

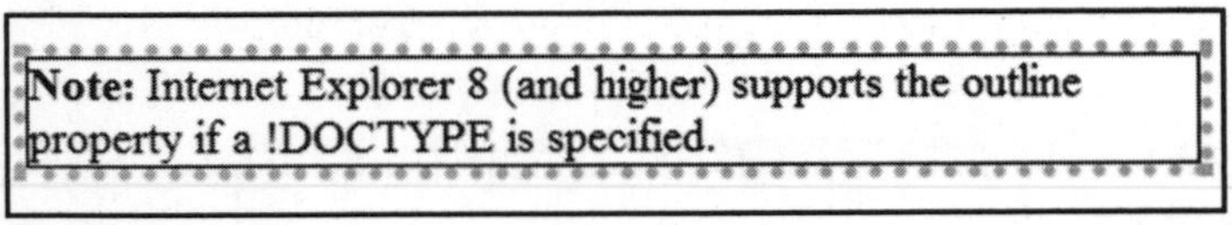

Note: Internet Explorer 8 (and higher) supports the outline
property if a !DOCTYPE is specified.

Figure 12.1

Outline Style

Use the outline-style property to set the style of an outline.

Try it yourself >>

```
<!DOCTYPE html PUBLIC "-//W3C//DTD XHTML 1.0 Transitional//
    EN" "http://www.w3.org/TR/xhtml1/DTD/xhtml1-transitional.
    dtd">
<html>
<head>
<style type="text/css">
    p {border:1px solid green;}
    p.dotted {outline-style:dotted;}
    p.dashed {outline-style:dashed;}
    p.solid {outline-style:solid;}
    p.double {outline-style:double;}
    p.groove {outline-style:groove;}
    p.ridge {outline-style:ridge;}
    p.inset {outline-style:inset;}
    p.outset {outline-style:outset;}
</style>
</head>
<body>

<p class="dotted">A dotted outline</p>
<p class="dashed">A dashed outline</p>
```

```
<p class="solid">A solid outline</p>
<p class="double">A double outline</p>
<p class="groove">A groove outline</p>
<p class="ridge">A ridge outline</p>
<p class="inset">An inset outline</p>
<p class="outset">An outset outline</p>
<b>Note:</b> Internet Explorer 8 (and higher) supports the
    outline properties if a !DOCTYPE is specified.
</body>
</html>
```

Figure 12.2 shows the result of this code.

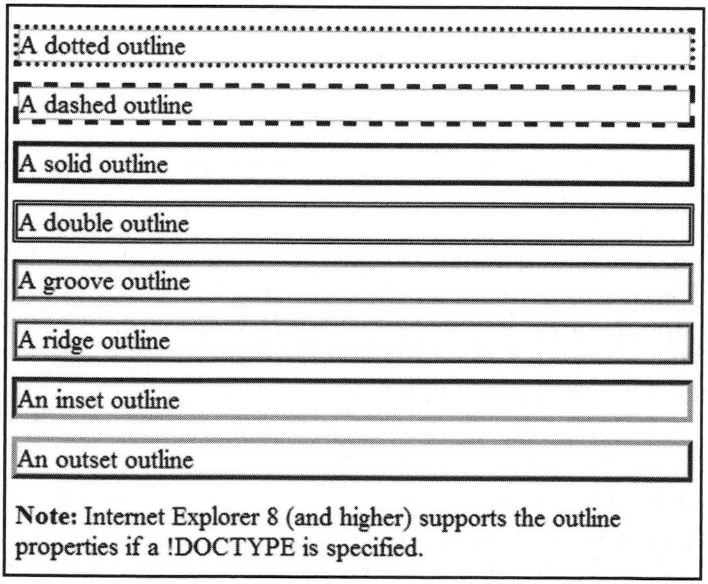

```
A dotted outline

A dashed outline

A solid outline

A double outline

A groove outline

A ridge outline

An inset outline

An outset outline
```

Note: Internet Explorer 8 (and higher) supports the outline properties if a !DOCTYPE is specified.

Figure 12.2

Outline Color

Use the outline-color property to set the color of an outline.

TIP   You can use a color name, an RGB value, or a hex value to specify the color of a border.

```
<!DOCTYPE html PUBLIC "-//W3C//DTD XHTML 1.0 Transitional//
  EN" "http://www.w3.org/TR/xhtml1/DTD/xhtml1-transitional.
  dtd">
<html>
<head>
<style type="text/css">
  p
  {
    border:1px solid black;
    outline-style:dotted;
    outline-color:#97C449;
  }
</style>
</head>

<body>
<p><b>Note:</b> Internet Explorer 8 (and higher) supports
  the outline properties if a !DOCTYPE is specified.</p>
</body>
</html>
```

Figure 12.3 shows the result of this code.

Note: Internet Explorer 8 (and higher) supports the outline
properties if a !DOCTYPE is specified.

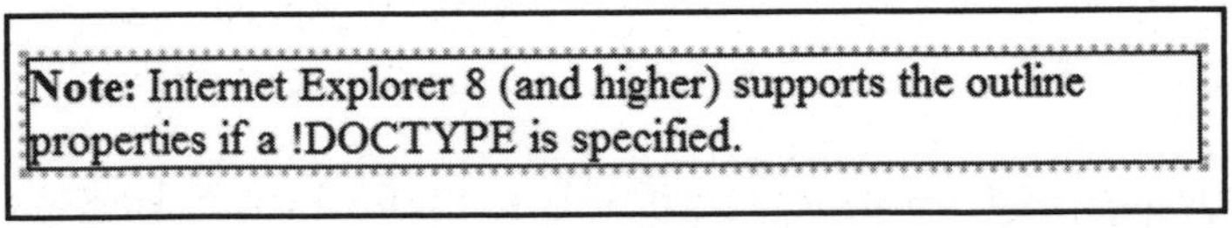

Figure 12.3

Outline Width

Use the outline-width property to set the width, or thickness, of an outline.

Figure 12.4 shows the result of this code.

Try it yourself >>

```
<!DOCTYPE html PUBLIC "-//W3C//DTD XHTML 1.0 Transitional//
   EN" "http://www.w3.org/TR/xhtml1/DTD/xhtml1-transitional.
   dtd">
<html>
<head>
<style type="text/css">
  p.one
  {
    border:1px solid green;
    outline-style:solid;
    outline-width:thin;
  }
  p.two
  {
    border:1px solid green;
    outline-style:dotted;
    outline-width:3px;
  }
</style>
</head>
<body>

<p class="one">This is some text in a paragraph.</p>
<p class="two">This is some text in a paragraph.</p>

<p><b>Note:</b> Internet Explorer 8 (and higher) supports
   the outline properties if a !DOCTYPE is specified.</p>
</body>
</html>
```

This is some text in a paragraph.

This is some text in a paragraph.

Note: Internet Explorer 8 (and higher) supports the outline properties if a !DOCTYPE is specified.

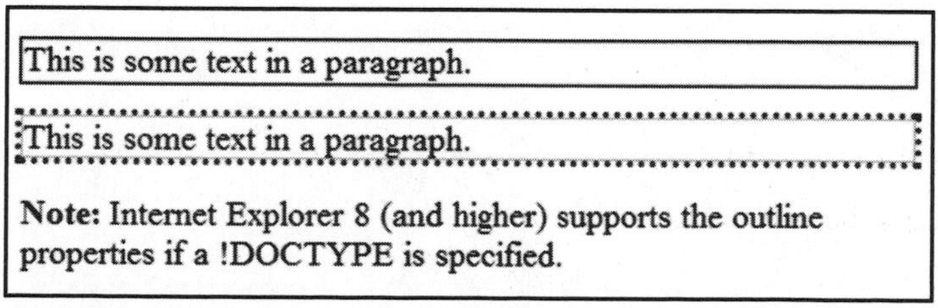

Figure 12.4

All CSS Outline Properties

The number in the CSS column indicates in which CSS version the property is defined (CSS1 or CSS2).

Property	Description	Values	CSS
outline	Sets all the outline properties in one declaration	*outline-color* *outline-style* *outline-width* inherit	2
outline-color	Sets the color of an outline	*color_name* *hex_number* *rgb_number* invert inherit	2
outline-style	Sets the style of an outline	none dotted dashed solid double groove ridge inset outset inherit	2
outline-width	Sets the width of an outline	thin medium thick *length* inherit	2

CHAPTER 13

CSS MARGIN

The CSS margin properties define the space around elements.

Margin

The margin clears an area around an element (outside the border). The margin does not have a background color and is completely transparent.

The top, right, bottom, and left margin can be changed independently using separate properties. A shorthand margin property can also be used to change all margins at once.

Possible Values

Value	Description
auto	The browser sets the margin. The result of this is dependent on the browser.
length	Defines a fixed margin (in pixels, pt, em, and so on)
%	Defines a margin in % of the containing element

TIP It is possible to use negative values to overlap content.

Individual Sides

In CSS, it is possible to specify different margins for different sides:

```
margin-top:100px;
margin-bottom:100px;
margin-right:50px;
margin-left:50px;
```

Figure 13.1 shows the result of this code.

```
<html>
<head>
<style type="text/css">
  p
  {
    background-color:green;
  }
  p.margin
  {
    margin-top:100px;
    margin-bottom:100px;
    margin-right:50px;
    margin-left:50px;
  }
</style>
</head>

<body>
<p>This is a paragraph with no specified margins.</p>
<p class="margin">This is a paragraph with specified mar-
  gins.</p>
</body>

</html>
```

This is a paragraph with no specified margins.

This is a paragraph with specified margins.

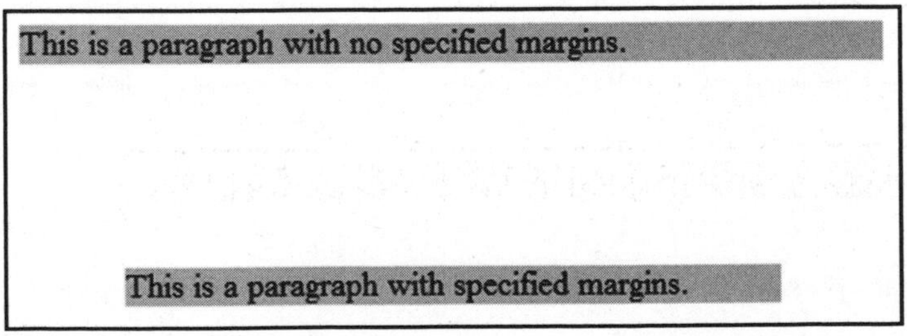

Figure 13.1

Shorthand Property

To shorten the code, it is possible to specify all the margin properties in one property. This is called a **shorthand property.**

The shorthand property for all the margin properties is `margin`:

```
margin:100px 50px;
```

Figure 13.2 shows the result of this code.

Try it yourself >>

```html
<html>
<head>
<style type="text/css">
  p
  {
    background-color:green;
  }
  p.margin
  {
    margin:100px 50px;
  }
</style>
</head>

<body>
<p>This is a paragraph with no specified margins.</p>
<p class="margin">This is a paragraph with specified
  margins.</p>
</body>

</html>
```

This is a paragraph with no specified margins.

This is a paragraph with specified margins.

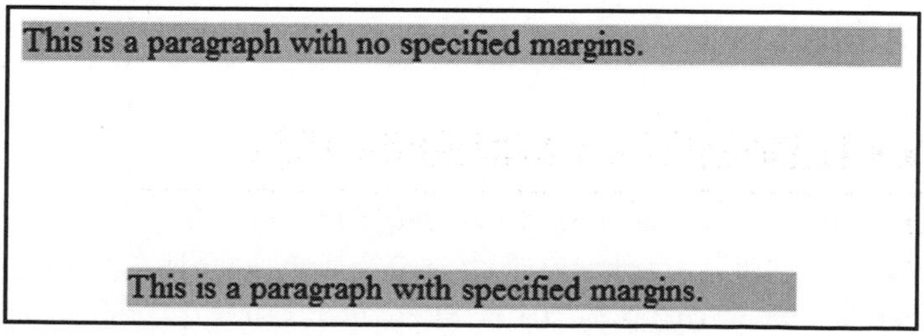

Figure 13.2

The `margin` property can have from one to four values.

▸▸ `margin:25px 50px 75px 100px;`

- Top margin is 25px.
- Right margin is 50px.
- Bottom margin is 75px.
- Left margin is 100px.

▸▸ `margin:25px 50px 75px;`

- Top margin is 25px.
- Right and left margins are 50px.
- Bottom margin is 75px.

▸▸ `margin:25px 50px;`

- Top and bottom margins are 25px.
- Right and left margins are 50px.

▸▸ `margin:25px;`

- All four margins are 25px.

Set the Top Margin

Use the `margin-top` property to set the top margin. This example uses a cm value.

Try it yourself >>

```
<html>
<head>
<style type="text/css">
  p.ex1 {margin-top:2cm;}
</style>
</head>

<body>

<p>A paragraph with no margins specified.</p>
<p class="ex1">A paragraph with a 2cm top margin.</p>
<p>A paragraph with no margins specified.</p>

</body>
</html>
```

Figure 13.3 shows the result of this code.

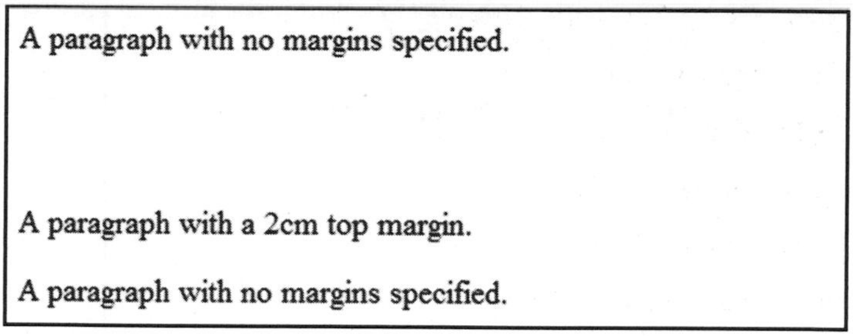

A paragraph with no margins specified.

A paragraph with a 2cm top margin.

A paragraph with no margins specified.

Figure 13.3

Set the Bottom Margin

Use the `margin-bottom` property to set the bottom margin. This example uses a percent value.

Try it yourself >>

```
<html>
<head>
<style type="text/css">
  p.bottommargin {margin-bottom:25%;}
</style>
</head>
<body>

<p>This is a paragraph with no margin specified.</p>
<p class="bottommargin">This is a paragraph with a specified
  bottom margin.</p>
<p>This is a paragraph with no margin specified.</p>

</body>
</html>
```

Figure 13.4 shows the result of this code.

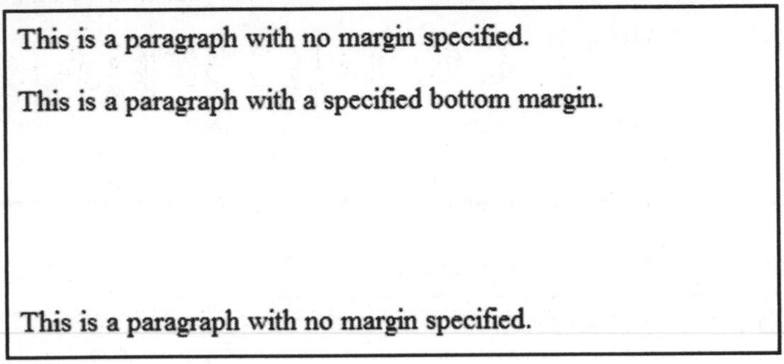

This is a paragraph with no margin specified.

This is a paragraph with a specified bottom margin.

This is a paragraph with no margin specified.

Figure 13.4

All CSS Margin Properties

The number in the CSS column indicates in which CSS version the property is defined (CSS1 or CSS2).

Property	Description	Values	CSS
margin	A shorthand property for setting the margin properties in one declaration	*margin-top* *margin-right* *margin-bottom* *margin-left*	1
margin-bottom	Sets the bottom margin of an element	auto *length* %	1
margin-left	Sets the left margin of an element	auto *length* %	1
margin-right	Sets the right margin of an element	auto *length* %	1
margin-top	Sets the top margin of an element	auto *length* %	1

CHAPTER 14

CSS PADDING

The CSS padding properties define the space between the element border and the element content.

Padding

The padding clears an area around the content (inside the border) of an element. The padding is affected by the background color of the element.

The top, right, bottom, and left padding can be changed independently using separate properties. A shorthand `padding` property can also be used to change all paddings at once.

Possible Values

Value	Description
length	Defines a fixed padding (in pixels, pt, em, and so on)
%	Defines a padding in % of the containing element

Individual Sides

In CSS, it is possible to specify different padding for different sides:

```
padding-top:25px;
padding-bottom:25px;
padding-right:50px;
padding-left:50px;
```

Figure 14.1 shows the result of this code.

Try it yourself >>

```
<html>
<head>
<style type="text/css">
  p
  {
    background-color:green;
  }
  p.padding
  {
    padding-top:25px;
    padding-bottom:25px;
    padding-right:50px;
    padding-left:50px;
  }
</style>
</head>

<body>
<p>This is a paragraph with no specified padding.</p>
<p class="padding">This is a paragraph with specified
  paddings.</p>
</body>

</html>
```

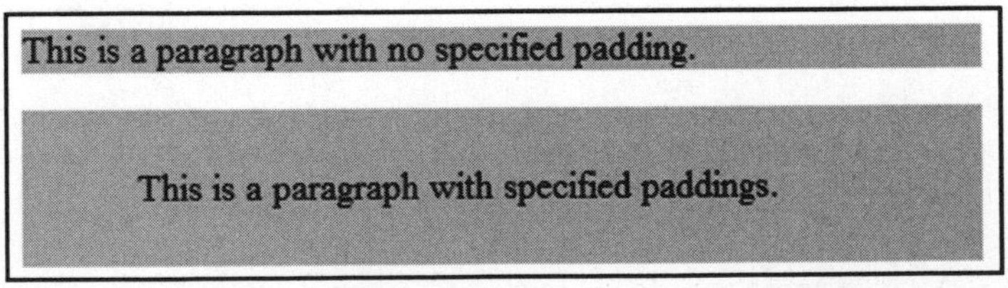

Figure 14.1

Shorthand Property

To shorten the code, it is possible to specify all the padding properties in one property. This is called a **shorthand property.**

The shorthand property for all the padding properties is `padding`:

```
padding:25px 50px;
```

Figure 14.2 shows the result of this code.

```
<html>
<head>
<style type="text/css">
  p
  {
    background-color:green;
  }
  p.padding
  {
    padding:25px 50px;
  }
</style>
</head>

<body>
<p>This is a paragraph with no specified padding.</p>
<p class="padding">This is a paragraph with specified
   paddings.</p>
</body>

</html>
```

This is a paragraph with no specified padding.

This is a paragraph with specified paddings.

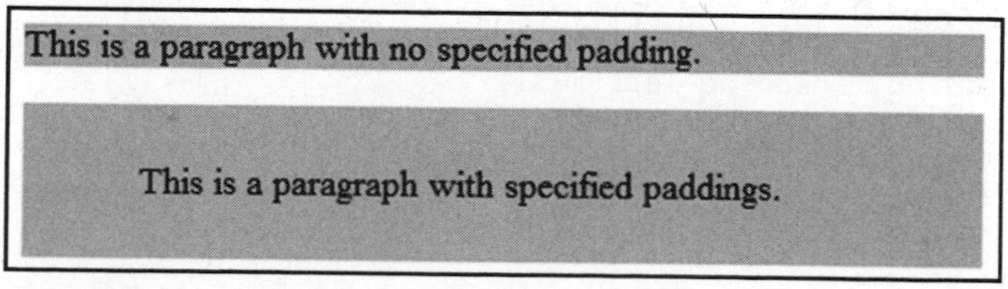

Figure 14.2

The padding property can have from one to four values.

▸▸ `padding:25px 50px 75px 100px;`

- Top padding is 25px.
- Right padding is 50px.
- Bottom padding is 75px.
- Left padding is 100px.

▸▸ `padding:25px 50px 75px;`

- Top padding is 25px.
- Right and left paddings are 50px.
- Bottom padding is 75px.

▸▸ `padding:25px 50px;`

- Top and bottom paddings are 25px.
- Right and left paddings are 50px.

▸▸ `padding:25px;`

- All four paddings are 25px.

Set Padding on Only One Side

You can set the padding for only one side of a **p** element using a length value or a percentage. This example demonstrates how to set the left padding using a centimeters value and a percentage.

Try it yourself >>

```
<html>
<head>
<style type="text/css">
  p.padding {padding-left:2cm;}
  p.padding2 {padding-left:50%;}
</style>
</head>

<body>
<p>This is a text with no left padding.</p>
<p class="padding">This text has a left padding of 2 cm.</p>
<p class="padding2">This text has a left padding of 50%.</p>
```

```
</body>
</html>
```

Figure 14.3 shows the result of this code.

This is a text with no left padding.

    This text has a left padding of 2 cm.

        This text has a left padding of 50%.

Figure 14.3

All CSS Padding Properties

The number in the CSS column indicates in which CSS version the property is defined (CSS1 or CSS2).

Property	Description	Values	CSS
padding	A shorthand property for setting all the padding properties in one declaration	*padding-top* *padding-right* *padding-bottom* *padding-left*	1
padding-bottom	Sets the bottom padding of an element	*length* *%*	1
padding-left	Sets the left padding of an element	*length* *%*	1
padding-right	Sets the right padding of an element	*length* *%*	1
padding-top	Sets the top padding of an element	*length* *%*	1

Section IV
CSS Layout

CHAPTER 15

CSS GROUPING AND NESTING SELECTORS

Grouping Selectors

In style sheets, there are often elements with the same style:

```
h1
{
  color:green;
}
h2
{
  color:green;
}
p
{
  color:green;
}
```

To minimize the code, you can group selectors.

Separate each selector with a comma.

In the following example, we have grouped the selectors from the previous code:

```
h1,h2,p
{
  color:green;
}
```

Figure 15.1 shows the result of this code.

```
<html>
<head>
<style type="text/css">
  h1,h2,p
  {
    color:green;
  }
</style>
</head>

<body>
<h1>Hello World!</h1>
<h2>Smaller heading!</h2>
<p>This is a paragraph.</p>
</body>
</html>
```

Hello World!

Smaller heading!

This is a paragraph.

Figure 15.1

Nesting Selectors

It is possible to apply a style for a selector within a selector.

In the following example, one style is specified for all p elements, and a separate style is specified for p elements nested within the marked class:

```
p
{
  color:green;
  text-align:center;
}
.marked
```

```
{
  background-color:green;
}
.marked p
{
  color:white;
}
```

Figure 15.2 shows the result of this code.

Try it yourself >>

```
<html>
<head>
<style type="text/css">
  p
  {
    color:green;
    text-align:center;
  }
  .marked
  {
    background-color:green;
  }
  .marked p
  {
    color:white;
  }
</style>
</head>

<body>
<p>This is a green, center-aligned paragraph.</p>
<div class="marked">
<p>The text in this is p element should not be green.</p>
</div>
<p>p elements inside a "marked" class element keep the
   alignment style but have a different text color.</p>
</body>
</html>
```

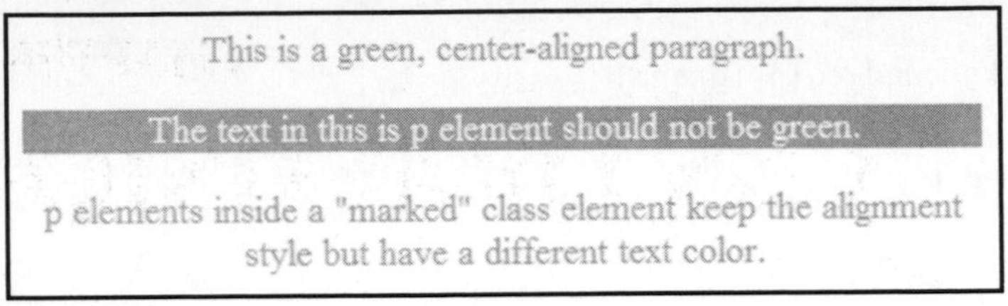

This is a green, center-aligned paragraph.

The text in this is p element should not be green.

p elements inside a "marked" class element keep the alignment style but have a different text color.

Figure 15.2

CHAPTER 16

CSS DIMENSION

The CSS dimension properties allow you to control the height and width of an element.

Height

Use the `height` property to set the height of different elements. Figure 16.1 shows the result of this code.

```
<html>
<head>
<style type="text/css">
  img.normal {height:auto}
  img.big {height:120px}
  p.ex
  {
    height:100px;
    width:100px;
  }
</style>
</head>

<body>
<img class="normal" src="logocss.gif" width="95" height="84"
  /><br />
<img class="big" src="logocss.gif" width="95" height="84" />

<p class="ex">The height and width of this paragraph is
  100px.</p>
```

(continued)

(continued)

```
<p>This paragraph doesn't have any height settings. This is
    some text in a paragraph. This is some text in a
    paragraph. This is some text in a paragraph.</p>
</body>
</html>
```

The height and
width of this
paragraph is
100px.

This paragraph doesn't have any height settings. This is some
text in a paragraph. This is some text in a paragraph. This is
some text in a paragraph.

Figure 16.1

Set Height Using Percent

You can also set the height of an element using a percent value. Figure 16.2 shows
the result of this code.

Try it yourself >>

```
<html>
<head>
<style type="text/css">
  img.normal {height:auto}
  img.big {height:50%}
  img.small {height:10%}
```

```
</style>
</head>

<body>
<img class="normal" src="logocss.gif" width="95" height="84"
  /><br />
<img class="big" src="logocss.gif" width="95" height="84"
  /><br />
<img class="small" src="logocss.gif" width="95" height="84"
  />
</body>
</html>
```

Figure 16.2

Width

Use the width property to set the width of an element. This example uses a pixel value. Figure 16.3 shows the result of this code.

Try it yourself >>

```
<html>
<head>
<style type="text/css">
  img
```

(continued)

(continued)

```
    {
       width: 200px
    }
  </style>
  </head>
  <body>

  <img src="logocss.gif" width="95" height="84" />

  </body>
  </html>
```

Figure 16.3

Maximum Height

Use the max-height property to set the maximum height of an element. Figure 16.4 shows the result of this code.

Try it yourself >>

```
<html>
<head>
<style type="text/css">
  img.normal {height:auto;}
  img.big {max-height:100px;}
  img.small {max-height:15px;}
</style>
</head>

<body>
<img class="normal" src="logocss.gif" width="95" height="84"
  /><br />
<img class="big" src="logocss.gif" width="95" height="84"
  /><br />
```

```
<img class="small" src="logocss.gif" width="95" height="84"
  />
</body>
</html>
```

Figure 16.4

Maximum Width

Use the `max-width` property to set the maximum width of an element. This example uses a percent value. Figure 16.5 shows the result of this code.

```
<html>
<head>
<style type="text/css">
  p
  {
    max-width: 50%
  }
</style>
</head>
<body>

<p>This is some text. This is some text. This is some text.
  This is some text. This is some text. This is some text.
  This is some text. This is some text. This is some text.
  </p>
```

(continued)

149

(continued)
```
  </body>
  </html>
```

This is some text. This is some
text. This is some text. This is
some text. This is some text.
This is some text. This is some
text. This is some text. This is
some text.

Figure 16.5

Minimum Height

Use the min-height property to set the minimum height of an element. This example uses pixel values. Figure 16.6 shows the result of this code.

```
<html>
<head>
<style type="text/css">
  img.normal {height:auto;}
  img.big {min-height:150px;}
  img.small {min-height:10px;}
</style>
</head>

<body>
<img class="normal" src="logocss.gif" width="95" height="84"
  /><br />
<img class="big" src="logocss.gif" width="95" height="84"
  /><br />
<img class="small" src="logocss.gif" width="95" height="84"
  />
</body>
</html>
```

150

Figure 16.6

All CSS Dimension Properties

The number in the CSS column indicates in which CSS version the property is defined (CSS1 or CSS2).

Property	Description	Values	CSS
height	Sets the height of an element	auto *length* % inherit	1
max-height	Sets the maximum height of an element	none *length* % inherit	2
max-width	Sets the maximum width of an element	none *length* % inherit	2
min-height	Sets the minimum height of an element	*length* % inherit	2
min-width	Sets the minimum width of an element	*length* % inherit	2
width	Sets the width of an element	auto *length* % inherit	1

CHAPTER 17

CSS DISPLAY AND VISIBILITY

The CSS classification properties specify if/how an element is to be displayed and control the visibility of an element as shown in Figure 17.1.

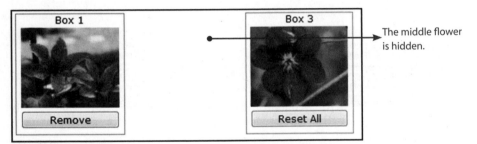

Figure 17.1

Hiding an Element—Two Methods

Hiding an element can be done by setting the display property to none or the visibility property to hidden. However, notice that these two methods produce different results:

visibility:hidden hides an element but it will still take up the same space as before. The element will be hidden but still affect the layout.

```
h1.hidden {visibility:hidden}
```

Figure 17.2 shows the result of this code.

```
<html>
<head>
<style type="text/css">
  h1.hidden {visibility:hidden}
</style>
</head>

<body>
<h1>This is a visible heading</h1>
<h1 class="hidden">This is a hidden heading</h1>
<p>Notice that the hidden heading still takes up space.</p>
</body>

</html>
```

This is a visible heading

Notice that the hidden heading still takes up space.

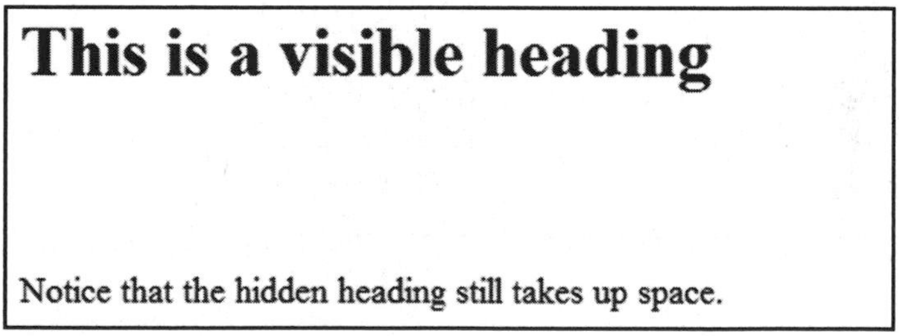

Figure 17.2

display:none hides an element, and it will not take up any space. The element will be hidden, and the page will be displayed as the element is not there.

Figure 17.3 shows the result of this code.

```
h1.hidden {display:none}
<html>
<head>
<style type="text/css">
  h1.hidden {display:none}
</style>
</head>
```

(continued)

(continued)

```
<body>
<h1>This is a visible heading</h1>
<h1 class="hidden">This is a hidden heading</h1>
<p>Notice that the hidden heading does not take up space.
  </p>
</body>

</html>
```

This is a visible heading

Notice that the hidden heading does not take up space.

Figure 17.3

CSS Display—Block and Inline Elements

A **block** element is an element that takes up the full width available and has a line break before and after it.

Examples of block elements:

```
<h1>
<p>
<div>
```

An **inline** element takes up only as much width as necessary and does not force line breaks.

Examples of inline elements:

```
<span>
<a>
```

Changing How an Element Is Displayed

Changing an inline element to a block element, or vice versa, can be useful for making the page look a specific way and still follow Web standards.

The following example displays list items as inline elements:

```
li {display:inline}
```

Figure 17.4 shows the result of this code.

Try it yourself >>

```
<html>
<head>
<style type="text/css">
  li{display:inline}
</style>
</head>
<body>

<p>Display this link list as a horizontal menu:</p>

<ul>
<li><a href="/html/default.asp" target="_blank">HTML</a>
    </li>
<li><a href="/css/default.asp" target="_blank">CSS</a></li>
<li><a href="/js/default.asp" target="_blank">JavaScript
    </a></li>
<li><a href="/xml/default.asp" target="_blank">XML</a></li>
</ul>

</body>
</html>
```

Display this link list as a horizontal menu:

     HTML CSS JavaScript XML

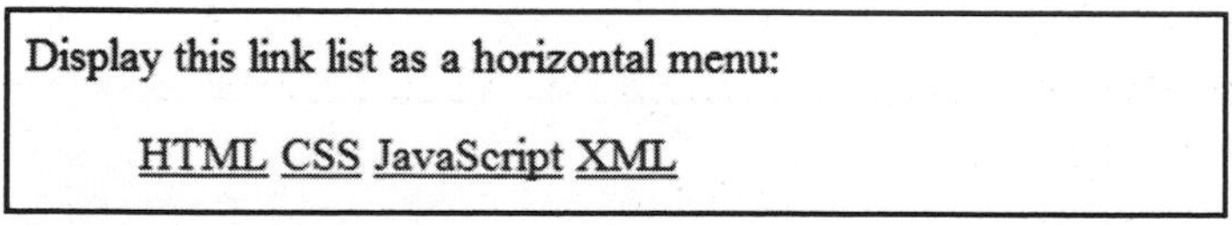

Figure 17.4

The following example displays span elements as block elements:

```
span {display:block}
```

Figure 17.5 shows the result of this code.

Try it yourself >>

```
<html>
<head>
<style type="text/css">
  span {display:block;}
</style>
</head>
<body>

<h2>Nirvana</h2>
<span>Record: MTV Unplugged in New York</span>
<span>Year: 1993</span>
<h2>Radiohead</h2>
<span>Record: OK Computer</span>
<span>Year: 1997</span>

</body>
</html>
```

Nirvana

Record: MTV Unplugged in New York
Year: 1993

Radiohead

Record: OK Computer
Year: 1997

Figure 17.5

N O T E Changing the display type of an element changes only how the element is displayed, *not* what kind of element it is. For example, an inline element set to display:block is not allowed to have a block element nested inside of it.

Hide a Table Element

Use `visibility:collapse` to hide a table element by collapsing it. Figure 17.6 shows the result of this code.

NOTE Internet Explorer supports `visibility:collapse` only if a `!DOCTYPE` is specified.

Try it yourself >>

```
<!DOCTYPE html PUBLIC "-//W3C//DTD XHTML 1.0 Transitional//
   EN" "http://www.w3.org/TR/xhtml1/DTD/xhtml1-transitional.
   dtd">
<html>
<head>
<style type="text/css">
  tr.collapse {visibility:collapse;}
</style>
</head>
<body>

<table border="1">
<tr>
<td>Peter</td>
<td>Griffin</td>
</tr>
<tr class="collapse">
<td>Lois</td>
<td>Griffin</td>
</tr>
<tr>
<td>Kathy</td>
<td>Griffin</td>
</tr>
</table>

</body>
</html>
```

157

Peter	Griffin
Kathy	Griffin

Figure 17.6

All CSS Classification Properties

The number in the CSS column indicates in which CSS version the property is defined (CSS1 or CSS2).

Property	Description	Values	CSS
display	Sets how/if an element is displayed	none inline block list-item run-in compact marker table inline-table table-row-group table-header-group table-footer-group table-row table-column-group table-column table-cell table-caption	1
visibility	Sets if an element should be visible or invisible	visible hidden collapse	2

CHAPTER 18

CSS POSITIONING

Decide which element to display in front!

Positioning can be tricky sometimes!

Elements can overlap!

Positioning

The CSS positioning properties allow you to position an element. You can also use them to place one element behind another and specify what should happen when an element's content is too big.

Elements can be positioned using the `top`, `bottom`, `left`, and `right` properties. However, these properties will not work unless the `position` property is set first. They also work differently depending on the positioning method.

There are four positioning methods: static, fixed, relative, and absolute.

Static Positioning

HTML elements are positioned static by default. A static positioned element is always positioned according to the normal flow of the page.

Static positioned elements are not affected by the `top`, `bottom`, `left`, and `right` properties.

Fixed Positioning

An element with fixed position is positioned relative to the browser window.

It will not move even if the window is scrolled:

```
p.pos_fixed
{
   position:fixed;
   top:30px;
```

```
      right:5px;
  }
```

Figure 18.1 shows the result of this code.

```
<!DOCTYPE html PUBLIC "-//W3C//DTD XHTML 1.0 Transitional//
  EN" "http://www.w3.org/TR/xhtml1/DTD/xhtml1-transitional.
  dtd">
<html>
<head>
<style type="text/css">
  p.pos_fixed
  {
    position:fixed;
    top:30px;
    right:5px;
  }
</style>
</head>
<body>

<p class="pos_fixed">Some more text</p>
<p><b>Note:</b> Internet Explorer 7 (and higher) supports
  the fixed value if a
!DOCTYPE is specified.</p>
<p>Some text</p><p>Some text</p><p>Some text</p><p>Some
  text</p><p>Some text</p><p>Some text</p><p>Some text</
  p><p>Some text</p><p>Some text</p><p>Some text</p><p>Some
  text</p><p>Some text</p><p>Some text</p><p>Some text</
  p><p>Some text</p><p>Some text</p>
</body>
</html>
```

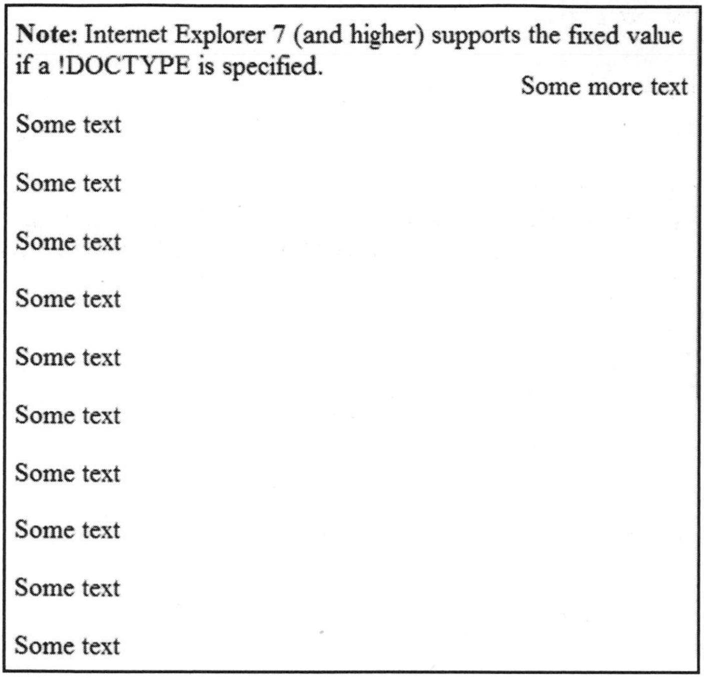

Note: Internet Explorer 7 (and higher) supports the fixed value if a !DOCTYPE is specified.

Some more text

Some text

Some text

Some text

Some text

Some text

Some text

Some text

Some text

Some text

Some text

Figure 18.1

NOTE Internet Explorer supports the fixed value only if a !DOCTYPE is specified.

Fixed position elements are removed from the normal flow. The document and other elements behave as if the fixed position element does not exist.

Fixed position elements can overlap other elements.

Relative Positioning

A relatively positioned element is positioned relative to its normal position.

```
h2.pos_left
{
  position:relative;
  left:-20px;
}
h2.pos_right
{
```

```
   position:relative;
   left:20px;
}
```

Figure 18.2 shows the result of this code.

```
<html>
<head>
<style type="text/css">
  h2.pos_left
  {
    position:relative;
    left:-20px;
  }

  h2.pos_right
  {
    position:relative;
    left:20px;
  }
</style>
</head>

<body>
<h2>This is a heading with no position</h2>
<h2 class="pos_left">This heading is moved left according to
   its normal position</h2>
<h2 class="pos_right">This heading is moved right according
   to its normal position</h2>
<p>Relative positioning moves an element RELATIVE to its
   original position.</p>
<p>The style "left:-20px" subtracts 20 pixels from the
   element's original left position.</p>
<p>The style "left:20px" adds 20 pixels to the element's
   original left position.</p>
</body>

</html>
```

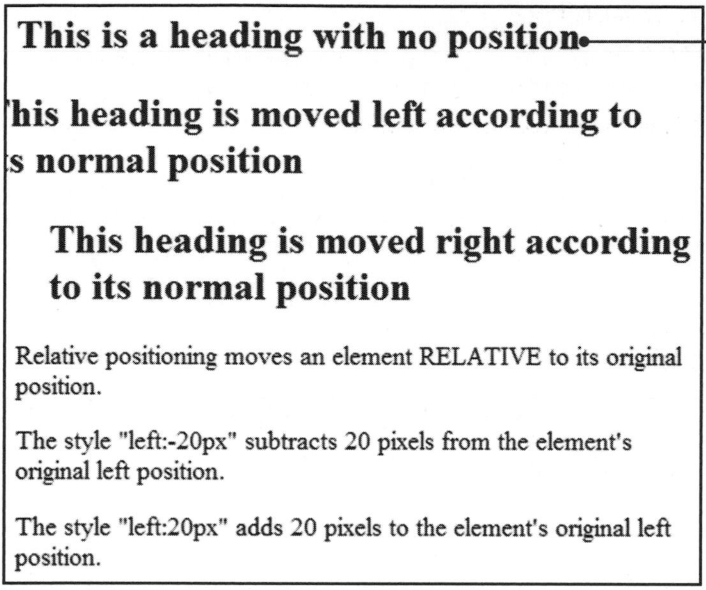

This is a heading with no position

> The text will not move as you scroll down the page.

his heading is moved left according to s normal position

This heading is moved right according to its normal position

Relative positioning moves an element RELATIVE to its original position.

The style "left:-20px" subtracts 20 pixels from the element's original left position.

The style "left:20px" adds 20 pixels to the element's original left position.

Figure 18.2

The content of relatively positioned elements can be moved and overlap other elements, but the reserved space for the element is still preserved in the normal flow.

```
h2.pos_top
{
  position:relative;
  top:-50px;
}
```

Figure 18.3 shows the result of this code.

Try it yourself >>

```
<html>
<head>
<style type="text/css">
  h2.pos_top
  {
    position:relative;
    top:-50px;
  }
</style>
</head>
```

(continued)

163

(continued)

```
<body>
<h2>This is a heading with no position</h2>
<h2 class="pos_top">This heading is moved upwards according
  to its normal position</h2>
<p><b>Note:</b> Even if the content of the relatively
  positioned element is moved, the reserved space for the
  element is still preserved in the normal flow.</p>
</body>


</html>
```

This is a heading with no position according to its normal position

Note: Even if the content of the relatively positioned element is moved, the reserved space for the element is still preserved in the normal flow.

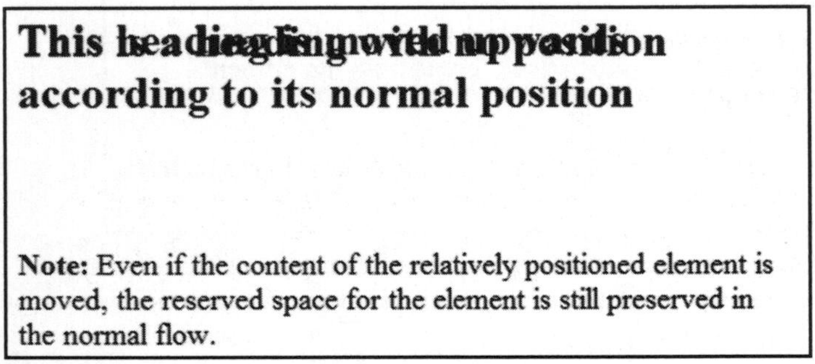

Figure 18.3

Relatively positioned elements are often used as container blocks for absolutely positioned elements.

Absolute Positioning

An absolute position element is positioned relative to the first parent element that has a position other than static. If no such element is found, the containing block is <html>:

```
h2
{
  position:absolute;
  left:100px;
  top:150px;
}
```

Figure 18.4 shows the result of this code.

```
<html>
<head>
<style type="text/css">
  h2
  {
    position:absolute;
    left:100px;
    top:150px;
  }
</style>
</head>

<body>
<h2>This is a heading with an absolute position</h2>
<p>With absolute positioning, an element can be placed
   anywhere on a page. The heading below is placed 100px from
   the left of the page and 150px from the top of the page.
   </p>
</body>

</html>
```

With absolute positioning, an element can be placed anywhere on a page. The heading below is placed 100px from the left of the page and 150px from the top of the page.

This is a heading with an absolute position

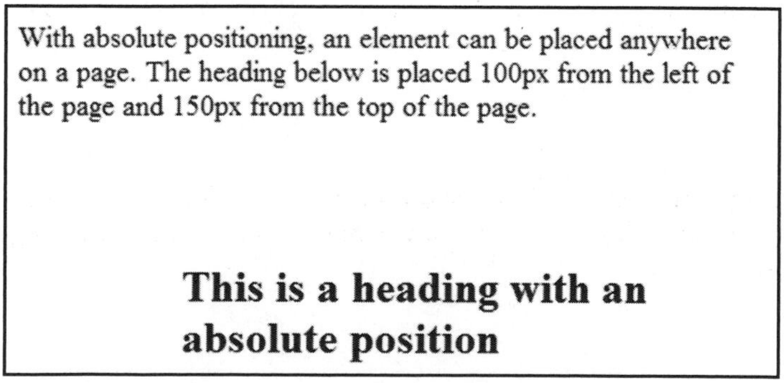

Figure 18.4

Absolutely positioned elements are removed from the normal flow. The document and other elements behave as if the absolutely positioned element does not exist.

Absolutely positioned elements can overlap other elements.

165

Overlapping Elements

When elements are positioned outside the normal flow, they can overlap other elements.

The z-index property specifies the stack order of an element (which element should be placed in front of, or behind, the others).

An element can have a positive or negative stack order:

```
img
{
    position:absolute;
    left:0px;
    top:0px;
    z-index:-1
}
```

Figure 18.5 shows the result of this code.

Try it yourself >>

```
<html>
<head>
<style type="text/css">
    img
    {
        position:absolute;
        left:0px;
        top:0px;
        z-index:-1;
    }
</style>
</head>

<body>
<h1>This is a heading</h1>
<img src="w3css.gif" width="100" height="140" />
<p>Because the image has a z-index of -1, it will be placed
    behind the text.</p>
</body>
</html>
```

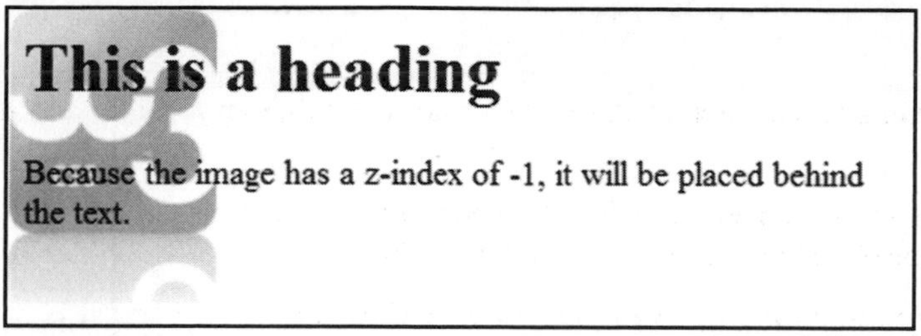

This is a heading

Because the image has a z-index of -1, it will be placed behind the text.

Figure 18.5

An element with greater stack order is always in front of an element with a lower stack order.

Additional Positioning Properties

CSS offers some additional properties to give you even more control over the design of your Web page.

Clip

What happens if an image is larger than its containing element? The `clip` property lets you specify the dimensions of an absolutely positioned element that should be visible, and the element is clipped into this shape and displayed. This example shows one way to use the `clip` property, and Figure 18.6 shows the result.

Try it yourself >>

```
<html>
<head>
<style type="text/css">
  img
  {
    position:absolute;
    clip:rect(0px,60px,200px,0px);
  }
</style>
</head>

<body>
<img src="w3css.gif" width="100" height="140" />
</body>
</html>
```

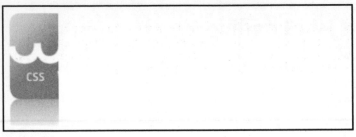

Figure 18.6

Overflow

The overflow property specifies what happens if content overflows an element's box. This example demonstrates how to set the browser to automatically handle overflow. This example shows one way to use the overflow property, and Figure 18.7 shows the result.

Try it yourself >>

```
<html>
<head>
<style type="text/css">
  div
  {
    background-color:#00FF00;
    width:150px;
    height:150px;
    overflow:auto;
  }
</style>
</head>

<body>
<p>The overflow property decides what to do if the content
   inside an element exceeds the given width and height
   properties.</p>
```

```
<div>
You can use the overflow property when you want to have
    better control of the layout. Try to change the overflow
    property to: visible, hidden, scroll, or inherit and see
    what happens. The default value is visible.
</div>
</body>

</html>
```

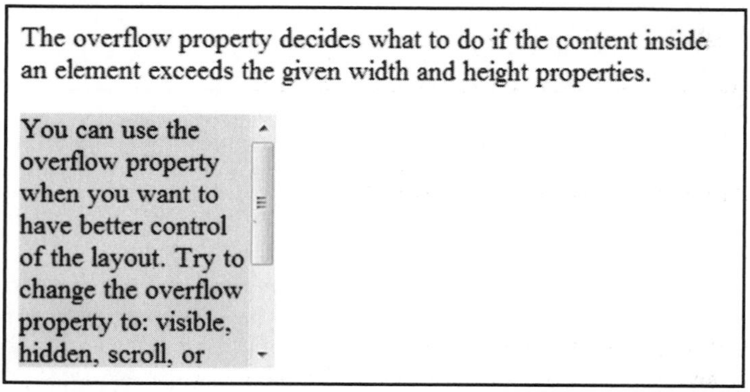

The overflow property decides what to do if the content inside
an element exceeds the given width and height properties.

You can use the
overflow property
when you want to
have better control
of the layout. Try to
change the overflow
property to: visible,
hidden, scroll, or

Figure 18.7

Use the overflow:scroll property to create a scroll bar when an element's content
is too big to fit in a specified area. Use the overflow:hidden property to hide any
content that overflows the box. See Figure 18.8 to see what this looks like.

Try it yourself >>

```
<html>
<head>
<style type="text/css">
  div.scroll
  {
    background-color:#00FFFF;
    width:100px;
    height:100px;
    overflow:scroll;
  }
```

(continued)

(continued)

```css
      div.hidden
      {
         background-color:#00FF00;
         width:100px;
         height:100px;
         overflow:hidden;
      }
   </style>
   </head>

   <body>
   <p>The overflow property specifies what to do if the content
      of an element exceeds the size of the element's box.</p>

   <p>overflow:scroll</p>
   <div class="scroll">You can use the overflow property when
      you want to have better control of the layout. The default
      value is visible.</div>

   <p>overflow:hidden</p>
   <div class="hidden">You can use the overflow property when
      you want to have better control of the layout. The default
      value is visible.</div>
   </body>
   </html>
```

The overflow property specifies what to do if the content of an element exceeds the size of the element's box.

overflow:scroll

> You can use
> the overflow
> property
> when you

overflow:hidden

> You can use
> the overflow
> property when
> you want to
> have better

Figure 18.8

Cursor

The cursor property specifies the type of cursor to be displayed when pointing on an element. This example lists all of the styles of cursor you can use.

 Figure 18.9 shows one of these cursors; to see all the options, please visit the w3schools Web page for this chapter, www.w3schools.com/css/css_positioning.asp, to experiment with all the options.

Try it yourself >>

```
<html>
<body>
<p>Mouse over the words to change the cursor.</p>
<span style="cursor:auto">auto</span><br />
<span style="cursor:crosshair">crosshair</span><br />
<span style="cursor:default">default</span><br />
<span style="cursor:e-resize">e-resize</span><br />
<span style="cursor:help">help</span><br />
<span style="cursor:move">move</span><br />
<span style="cursor:n-resize">n-resize</span><br />
<span style="cursor:ne-resize">ne-resize</span><br />
```

(continued)

171

(continued)

```
<span style="cursor:nw-resize">nw-resize</span><br />
<span style="cursor:pointer">pointer</span><br />
<span style="cursor:progress">progress</span><br />
<span style="cursor:s-resize">s-resize</span><br />
<span style="cursor:se-resize">se-resize</span><br />
<span style="cursor:sw-resize">sw-resize</span><br />
<span style="cursor:text">text</span><br />
<span style="cursor:w-resize">w-resize</span><br />
<span style="cursor:wait">wait</span><br />
</body>
</html>
```

Mouse over the words to change the cursor.

auto
crosshair
default
e-resize
help
move
n-resize
ne-resize
nw-resize
pointer
progress
s-resize
se-resize
sw-resize
text
w-resize
wait

Figure 18.9

All CSS Positioning Properties

The number in the CSS column indicates in which CSS version the property is defined (CSS1 or CSS2).

Property	Description	Values	CSS
bottom	Sets the bottom margin edge for a positioned box	auto *length* % inherit	2

172

Property	Description	Value	CSS
clip	Clips an absolutely positioned element	*shape* auto inherit	2
cursor	Specifies the type of cursor to be displayed	*url* auto crosshair default pointer move e-resize ne-resize nw-resize n-resize se-resize sw-resize s-resize w-resize text wait help	2
left	Sets the left margin edge for a positioned box	auto *length* % inherit	2
overflow	Specifies what happens if content overflows an element's box	auto hidden scroll visible inherit	2
position	Specifies the type of positioning for an element	absolute fixed relative static inherit	2
right	Sets the right margin edge for a positioned box	auto *length* % inherit	2
top	Sets the top margin edge for a positioned box	auto *length* % inherit	2
z-index	Sets the stack order of an element	*number* auto inherit	2

CHAPTER 19

CSS FLOAT

With CSS float, an element can be pushed to the left or right, allowing other elements to wrap around it.

Float is very often used for images, but it is also useful when working with layouts.

How Elements Float

Elements are floated horizontally, which means that an element can only be floated left or right, not up or down.

A floated element will move as far to the left or right as it can. Usually this means all the way to the left or right of the containing element.

The elements after the floating element will flow around it.

The elements before the floating element will not be affected.

If an image is floated to the right, text that follows flows around it to the left:

```
img
{
  float:right;
}
```

Figure 19.1 shows the result of this code.

Try it yourself >>

```
<html>
<head>
<style type="text/css">
  img
  {
    float:right;
  }
</style>
</head>
```

```
<body>
<p>In the paragraph below, we have added an image with style
  <b>float:right</b>. The result is that the image will float
  to the right in the paragraph.</p>
<p>
<img src="logocss.gif" width="95" height="84" />
This is some text. This is some text. This is some text.
This is some text. This is some text. This is some text.
This is some text. This is some text. This is some text.
This is some text. This is some text. This is some text.
This is some text. This is some text. This is some text.
This is some text. This is some text. This is some text.
This is some text. This is some text. This is some text.
This is some text. This is some text. This is some text.
This is some text. This is some text. This is some text.
This is some text. This is some text. This is some text.
</p>
</body>

</html>
```

In the paragraph below, we have added an image with style **float:right**. The result is that the image will float to the right in the paragraph.

This is some text. This is some text.

Figure 19.1

Floating Elements Next to Each Other

If you place several floating elements after each other, they will float next to each other if there is room.

Here we have made an image gallery using the **float** property:

```
.thumbnail
{
  float:left;
  width:110px;
  height:90px;
  margin:5px;
}
```

Figure 19.2 shows the result of this code.

Try it yourself >>

```
<html>
<head>
<style type="text/css">
  .thumbnail
  {
    float:left;
    width:110px;
    height:90px;
    margin:5px;
  }
</style>
</head>

<body>
<h3>Image Gallery</h3>
<p>Try resizing the window to see what happens when the
  images do not have enough room.</p>
<img class="thumbnail" src="klematis_small.jpg" width="107"
  height="90">
<img class="thumbnail" src="klematis2_small.jpg" width="107"
  height="80">
<img class="thumbnail" src="klematis3_small.jpg" width="116"
  height="90">
<img class="thumbnail" src="klematis4_small.jpg" width="120"
  height="90">
```

```
<img class="thumbnail" src="klematis_small.jpg" width="107"
  height="90">
<img class="thumbnail" src="klematis2_small.jpg" width="107"
  height="80">
<img class="thumbnail" src="klematis3_small.jpg" width="116"
  height="90">
<img class="thumbnail" src="klematis4_small.jpg" width="120"
  height="90">
</body>
</html>
```

Figure 19.2

Turning Off Float—Using Clear

Elements after the floating element will flow around it. To avoid this, use the clear property.

The clear property specifies on which sides of an element other floating elements are not allowed.

Add a text line into the image gallery using the `clear` property:

```
.text_line
{
  clear:both;
}
```

Figure 19.3 shows the result of this code.

```
<html>
<head>
<style type="text/css">
  .thumbnail
  {
    float:left;
    width:110px;
    height:90px;
    margin:5px;
  }
  .text_line
  {
    clear:both;
    margin-bottom:2px;
  }
</style>
</head>

<body>
<h3>Image Gallery</h3>
<p>Try resizing the window to see what happens when the
   images do not have enough room.</p>
<img class="thumbnail" src="klematis_small.jpg" width="107"
   height="90">
<img class="thumbnail" src="klematis2_small.jpg" width="107"
   height="80">
<img class="thumbnail" src="klematis3_small.jpg" width="116"
   height="90">
<img class="thumbnail" src="klematis4_small.jpg" width="120"
   height="90">
<h3 class="text_line">Second row</h3>
<img class="thumbnail" src="klematis_small.jpg" width="107"
   height="90">
```

```
<img class="thumbnail" src="klematis2_small.jpg" width="107"
   height="80">
```

```
<img class="thumbnail" src="klematis3_small.jpg" width="116"
   height="90">
```

```
<img class="thumbnail" src="klematis4_small.jpg" width="120"
   height="90">
```

```
</body>
```

```
</html>
```

Figure 19.3

More Things You Can Do with Float

By combining float with other CSS properties, you can create sophisticated layouts on your Web page.

Add a Caption and a Border

Let an image with a caption float to the right, as shown in Figure 19.4.

Try it yourself >>

```
<html>
<head>
```

(continued)

(continued)

```
<style type="text/css">
  div
  {
    float:right;
    width:120px;
    margin:0 0 15px 20px;
    padding:15px;
    border:1px solid black;
    text-align:center;
  }
</style>
</head>

<body>
<div>
<img src="logocss.gif" width="95" height="84" /><br />
CSS is fun!
</div>
<p>
This is some text. This is some text. This is some text.
This is some text. This is some text. This is some text.
This is some text. This is some text. This is some text.
This is some text. This is some text. This is some text.
This is some text. This is some text. This is some text.
This is some text. This is some text. This is some text.
This is some text. This is some text. This is some text.
This is some text. This is some text. This is some text.
This is some text. This is some text. This is some text.
</p>

<p>
In the paragraph above, the div element is 120 pixels wide
  and it contains the image.
The div element floats to the right.
The div has margins added to push the text away.
Borders and padding are added to the div to frame the
  picture and the caption.
</p>
</body>

</html>
```

This is some text. This is some text. This is some text. This is some text. This is some text. This is some text. This is some text. This is some text. This is some text. This is some text. This is some text. This is some text. This is some text. This is some text. This is some text. This is some text.

CSS is fun!

This is some text. This is some text. This is some text. This is some text. This is some text. This is some text. This is some text. This is some text. This is some text. This is some text. This is some text. This is some text.

In the paragraph above, the div element is 120 pixels wide and it contains the image. The div element floats to the right. The div has margins added to push the text away. Borders and padding are added to the div to frame the picture and the caption.

Figure 19.4

Create a Fancy First Letter

Let the first letter of a paragraph float to the left and style the letter, as shown in Figure 19.5.

Try it yourself >>

```
<html>
<head>
<style type="text/css">
  span
  {
    float:left;
    width:0.7em;
    font-size:400%;
    font-family:algerian,courier;
    line-height:80%;
  }
</style>
</head>

<body>
```

(continued)

(continued)

```
<p>
<span>T</span>his is some text.
This is some text. This is some text.
This is some text. This is some text. This is some text.
This is some text. This is some text. This is some text.
This is some text. This is some text. This is some text.
This is some text. This is some text. This is some text.
This is some text. This is some text. This is some text.
This is some text. This is some text. This is some text.
</p>


<p>
In the paragraph above, the first letter of the text is
    embedded in a span element.
The span element has a width that is 0.7 times the size of
    the current font.
The font-size of the span element is 400% (quite large) and
    the line-height is 80%.
The font of the letter in the span will be in "Algerian".
</p>

</body>
</html>
```

Figure 19.5

Create a Homepage without Tables

Use float to create a homepage with a header, footer, left content, and main content, as shown in Figure 19.6.

Try it yourself >>

```
<html>
<head>
<style type="text/css">
  div.container
  {
    width:100%;
    margin:0px;
    border:1px solid gray;
    line-height:125%;
  }
  div.header,div.footer
  {
    padding:0.5em;
    color:white;
    background-color:gray;
    clear:left;
  }
  h1.header
  {
    padding:0;
    margin:0;
  }
  div.left
  {
    float:left;
    width:160px;
    margin:0;
    padding:1em;
  }
  div.content
  {
    margin-left:190px;
    border-left:1px solid gray;
    padding:1em;
```

(continued)

183

(continued)

```
      }
    </style>
    </head>
    <body>

    <div class="container">
    <div class="header"><h1 class="header">w3schools.com</h1>
      </div>
    <div class="left"><p>"Never increase, beyond what is
      necessary, the number of entities required to explain
      anything." William of Ockham (1285-1349)</p></div>
    <div class="content">
    <h2>Free Web Building Tutorials</h2>
    <p>At w3schools you will find all the Web-building tutorials
      you need.</p>
    <p>w3schools - The Largest Web Developers' Site On The
      Net!</p></div>
    <div class="footer">Copyright 1999-2010 by Refsnes Data.
      </div>
    </div>

    </body>
    </html>
```

Figure 19.6

All CSS Float Properties

The number in the CSS column indicates in which CSS version the property is defined (CSS1 or CSS2).

Property	Description	Values	CSS
clear	Specifies which sides of an element where other floating elements are not allowed	left right both none inherit	1
float	Specifies whether or not a box should float	left right none inherit	1

CHAPTER 20

CSS HORIZONTAL ALIGN

> In CSS, several properties are used to align elements horizontally.

Aligning Block Elements

A block element is an element that takes up the full width available and has a line break before and after it.

Examples of block elements:

» `<h1>`

» `<p>`

» `<div>`

For more on aligning text, see Chapter 5, "Styling Text."

In this chapter, we show you how to horizontally align block elements for layout purposes.

Center Aligning Using the Margin Property

Block elements can be aligned by setting the left and right margins to `auto`.

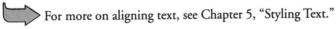

NOTE Using `margin: auto` will not work in Internet Explorer unless a `!DOCTYPE` is declared. See the section "Cross-Browser Compatibility Issues" later in this chapter for a cross-browser fix.

Setting the left and right margins to `auto` specifies that they should split the available margin equally. The result is a centered element, as shown in Figure 20.1.

```css
.center
{
  margin-left:auto;
  margin-right:auto;
  width:70%;
  background-color:#b0e0e6;
}
```

```html
<!DOCTYPE html PUBLIC "-//W3C//DTD XHTML 1.0 Transitional//
  EN" "http://www.w3.org/TR/xhtml1/DTD/xhtml1-transitional.
  dtd">
<html>
<head>
<style type="text/css">
  .center
  {
    margin:auto;
    width:70%;
    background-color:#b0e0e6;
  }
</style>
</head>

<body>
<div class="center">
<p>In my younger and more vulnerable years my father gave me
  some advice that I've been turning over in my mind ever
  since.</p>
<p>"Whenever you feel like criticizing anyone," he told me,
  "just remember that all the people in this world haven't
  had the advantages that you've had."</p>
</div>
<p><b>Note: </b>Using margin:auto will not work in Internet
  Explorer, unless a !DOCTYPE is declared.</p>
</body>
</html>
```

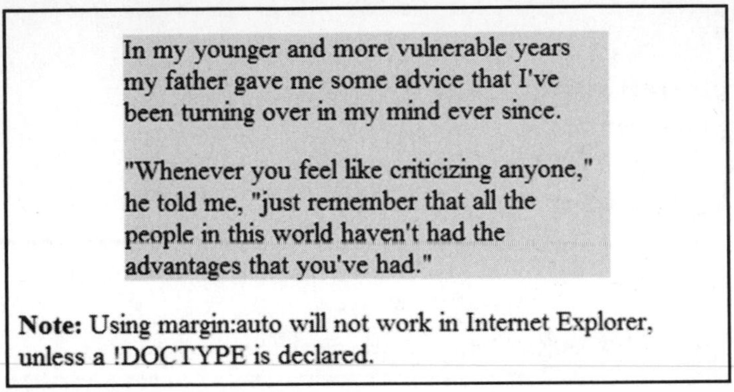

In my younger and more vulnerable years
my father gave me some advice that I've
been turning over in my mind ever since.

"Whenever you feel like criticizing anyone,"
he told me, "just remember that all the
people in this world haven't had the
advantages that you've had."

Note: Using margin:auto will not work in Internet Explorer,
unless a !DOCTYPE is declared.

Figure 20.1

TIP   Aligning has no effect if the width is 100%.

Cross-Browser Compatibility Issues

There is a bug in Internet Explorer's handling of margins for block elements.

In IE, block elements are sometimes treated as inline content. This is particularly problematic when it comes to centering.

For centering to work in IE, use the `text-align` property.

To avoid this affecting the text in the original <div>, add a new <div> as a container with `text-align:center` and reset the `text-align` in the original <div>. Figure 20.2 shows the result of this code.

```
.container
{
  text-align:center;
}
.center
{
  margin-left:auto;
  margin-right:auto;
  width:70%;
  background-color:#b0e0e6;
  text-align:left;
}
```

Now the code for centering a block element works in all browsers!

Try it yourself >>

```
<html>
<head>
<style type="text/css">
  .container
  {
    text-align:center;
  }
  .center
  {
    margin-left:auto;
    margin-right:auto;
    width:70%;
    background-color:#b0e0e6;
    text-align:left;
  }
</style>
</head>

<body>
<div class="container">
<div class="center">
<p>In my younger and more vulnerable years my father gave me
   some advice that I've been turning over in my mind ever
   since.</p>
<p>"whenever you feel like criticizing anyone," he told me,
   "just remember that all the people in this world haven't
   had the advantages that you've had."</p>
</div>
</div>


<p><b>Note:</b> In IE 5 there is a margin handling bug for
   block elements. Block elements are sometimes treated as
   inline content. This is particularly problematic when it
   comes to centering.
For centering to work in IE5, use the text-align property,
   as in this example.</p>


</body>
</html>
```

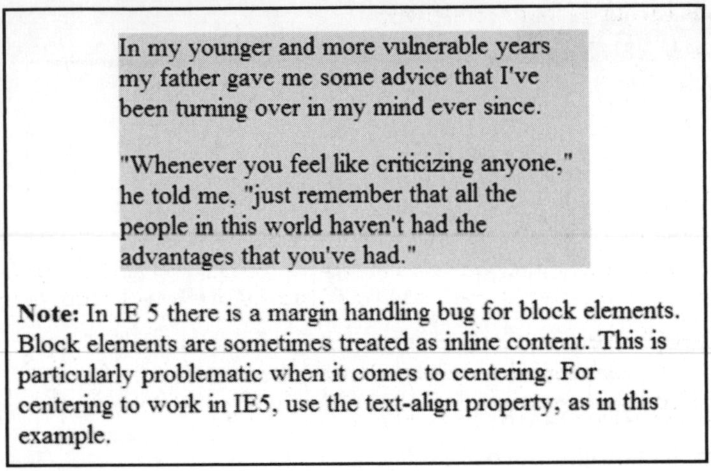

> In my younger and more vulnerable years
> my father gave me some advice that I've
> been turning over in my mind ever since.
>
> "Whenever you feel like criticizing anyone,"
> he told me, "just remember that all the
> people in this world haven't had the
> advantages that you've had."

Note: In IE 5 there is a margin handling bug for block elements. Block elements are sometimes treated as inline content. This is particularly problematic when it comes to centering. For centering to work in IE5, use the text-align property, as in this example.

Figure 20.2

Left and Right Aligning Using the Position Property

One method of aligning elements is to use absolute positioning, as shown in Figure 20.3.

```
.right
{
  position:absolute;
  right:0px;
  width:300px;
  background-color:#b0e0e6;
}
```

Try it yourself >>

```
<html>
<head>
<style type="text/css">
  .right
  {
    position:absolute;
    right:0px;
    width:300px;
```

```
        background-color:#b0e0e6;
    }
</style>
</head>

<body>
<div class="right">
<p>In my younger and more vulnerable years my father gave me
    some advice that I've been turning over in my mind ever
    since.</p>
<p>"Whenever you feel like criticizing anyone," he told me,
    "just remember that all the people in this world haven't
    had the advantages that you've had."</p>
</div>
</body>
</html>
</html>
```

In my younger and more vulnerable years my father gave me some advice that I've been turning over in my mind ever since.

"Whenever you feel like criticizing anyone," he told me, "just remember that all the people in this world haven't had the advantages that you've had."

Figure 20.3

> **NOTE** Absolute positioned elements are removed from the normal flow and can overlap elements.

Cross-Browser Compatibility Issues

When aligning elements like this, it is always a good idea to predefine margin and padding for the <body> element. This is to avoid visual differences in different browsers.

There is also another problem with IE when using the position property. If a container element (in our case <div class="container">) has a specified width, and the !DOCTYPE declaration is missing, IE will add a 17 pixel margin on the

191

right side. This seems to be space reserved for a scrollbar. Always set the !DOCTYPE declaration when using the position property. Figure 20.4 shows the result of this code.

```css
body
{
  margin:0;
  padding:0;
}
.container
{
  position:relative;
  width:100%
}
.right
{
  position:absolute;
  right:0px;
  width:300px;
  background-color:#b0e0e6;
}
```

Try it yourself >>

```html
<!DOCTYPE html PUBLIC "-//W3C//DTD XHTML 1.0 Transitional//
  EN" "http://www.w3.org/TR/xhtml1/DTD/xhtml1-transitional.
  dtd">
<html>
<head>
<style type="text/css">
  body
  {
    margin:0;
    padding:0;
  }
  .container
  {
    position:relative;
    width:100%;
  }
  .right
  {
    position:absolute;
```

```
        right:0px;
        width:300px;
        background-color:#b0e0e6;
    }
</style>
</head>
<body>
<div class="container">
<div class="right">
<p><b>Note: </b>When aligning using the position property,
    always include the !DOCTYPE declaration! If missing, it
    can produce strange results in IE browsers.</p>
</div>
</div>

</body>
</html>
```

> **Note:** When aligning using the position property, always include the !DOCTYPE declaration! If missing, it can produce strange results in IE browsers.

Figure 20.4

Left and Right Aligning Using the Float Property

One method of aligning elements is to use the float property:

```
.right
{
  float:right;
  width:300px;
  background-color:#b0e0e6;
}
```

Figure 20.5 shows the result of this code.

193

Try it yourself >>

```html
<html>
<head>
<style type="text/css">
  .right
  {
    float:right;
    width:300px;
    background-color:#b0e0e6;
  }
</style>
</head>

<body>
<div class="right">
<p>In my younger and more vulnerable years my father gave me
  some advice that I've been turning over in my mind ever
  since.</p>
<p>"Whenever you feel like criticizing anyone," he told me,
  "just remember that all the people in this world haven't
  had the advantages that you've had."</p>
</div>
</body>
</html>
```

In my younger and more vulnerable years my father gave me some advice that I've been turning over in my mind ever since.

"Whenever you feel like criticizing anyone," he told me, "just remember that all the people in this world haven't had the advantages that you've had."

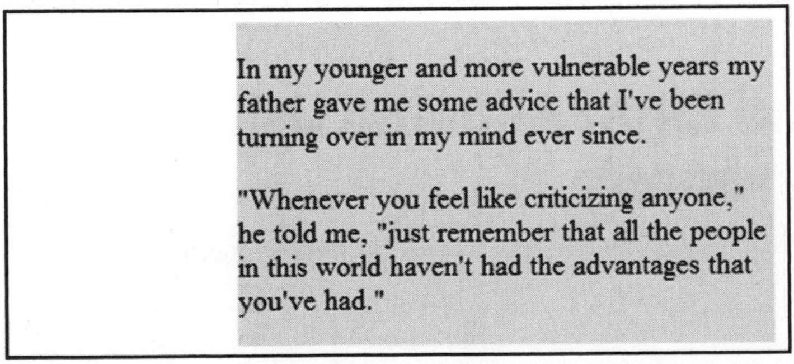

Figure 20.5

Cross-Browser Compatibility Issues

When aligning elements like this, it is always a good idea to predefine `margin` and `padding` for the `<body>` element. This is to avoid visual differences in different browsers.

There is also another problem with IE when using the **float** property. If the `!DOC-TYPE` declaration is missing, IE will add a 17 pixel margin on the right side. This seems to be space reserved for a scrollbar. Always set the `!DOCTYPE` declaration when using the **float** property:

```css
body
{
  margin:0;
  padding:0;
}
.right
{
  float:right;
  width:300px;
  background-color:#b0e0e6;
}
```

Figure 20.6 shows the result of this code.

```html
<!DOCTYPE html PUBLIC "-//W3C//DTD XHTML 1.0 Transitional//
    EN" "http://www.w3.org/TR/xhtml1/DTD/xhtml1-transitional.
    dtd">
<html>
<head>
<style type="text/css">
  body
  {
    margin:0;
    padding:0;
  }
  .right
  {
    float:right;
    width:300px;
    background-color:#b0e0e6;
  }
```

(continued)

195

(continued)

```
    </style>
    </head>
    <body>
    <div class="right">
    <p><b>Note: </b>When aligning using the float property,
      always include the !DOCTYPE declaration! If missing, it
      can produce strange results in IE browsers.</p>
    </div>

    </body>
    </html>
```

Note: When aligning using the float property, always include the !DOCTYPE declaration! If missing, it can produce strange results in IE browsers.

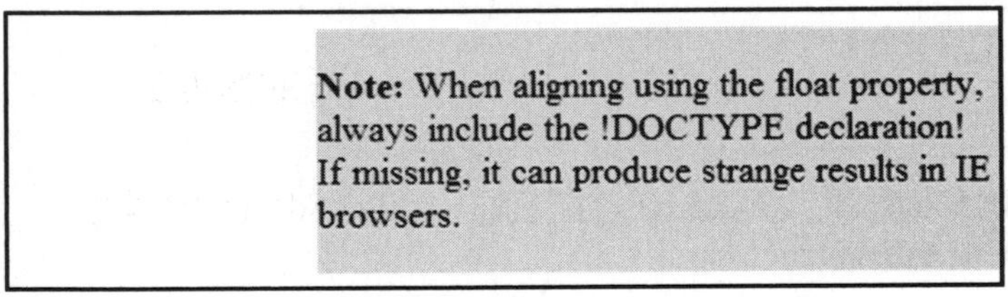

Figure 20.6

Section V
CSS Advanced

CHAPTER 21

CSS PSEUDO-CLASSES

CSS pseudo-classes are used to add special effects to some selectors.

Syntax

The syntax of pseudo-classes:

```
selector:pseudo-class {property:value}
```

CSS classes can also be used with pseudo-classes:

```
selector.class:pseudo-class {property:value}
```

Anchor Pseudo-Classes

Links can be displayed in different ways in a CSS-supporting browser. Figure 21.1 shows a selected link.

```
a:link {color:#FF0000}        /* unvisited link */
a:visited {color:#00FF00}     /* visited link */
a:hover {color:#FF00FF}       /* mouse over link */
a:active {color:#0000FF}      /* selected link */
```

Try it yourself >>

```
<html>
<head>
<style type="text/css">
  a:link {color:#FF0000;}     /* unvisited link */
  a:visited {color:#00FF00;}  /* visited link */
  a:hover {color:#FF00FF;}    /* mouse over link */
  a:active {color:#0000FF;}   /* selected link */
```

(continued)

199

(continued)

```
        </style>
        </head>

        <body>
        <p><b><a href="default.asp" target="_blank">This is a link
            </a></b></p>
        <p><b>Note:</b> a:hover MUST come after a:link and a:visited
            in the CSS definition in order to be effective.</p>
        <p><b>Note:</b> a:active MUST come after a:hover in the CSS
            definition in order to be effective.</p>
        </body>
        </html>
```

This is a link

Note: a:hover MUST come after a:link and a:visited in the CSS definition in order to be effective.

Note: a:active MUST come after a:hover in the CSS definition in order to be effective.

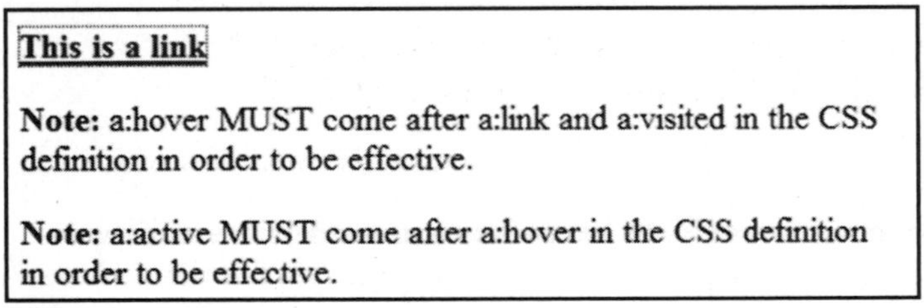

Figure 21.1

NOTE Pseudo-class names are not case-sensitive.

More Hyperlink Styles

You can use pseudo-classes to change more than just the colors of hyperlinks. This example shows how to add other styles to hyperlinks. Figure 21.2 shows the results of the code and is modified to show how each link looks on mouseover.

Try it yourself >>

```
<html>
<head>
<style type="text/css">
  a.one:link {color:#ff0000;}
  a.one:visited {color:#0000ff;}
  a.one:hover {color:#ffcc00;}
```

```
a.two:link {color:#ff0000;}
a.two:visited {color:#0000ff;}
a.two:hover {font-size:150%;}

a.three:link {color:#ff0000;}
a.three:visited {color:#0000ff;}
a.three:hover {background:#66ff66;}

a.four:link {color:#ff0000;}
a.four:visited {color:#0000ff;}
a.four:hover {font-family:monospace;}

a.five:link {color:#ff0000;text-decoration:none;}
a.five:visited {color:#0000ff;text-decoration:none;}
a.five:hover {text-decoration:underline;}
</style>
</head>

<body>
<p>Mouse over the links to see them change layout.</p>

<p><b><a class="one" href="default.asp" target="_blank">This
link changes color</a></b></p>
<p><b><a class="two" href="default.asp" target="_blank">This
link changes font-size</a></b></p>
<p><b><a class="three" href="default.asp" target=
"_blank">This link changes background-color</a></b></p>
<p><b><a class="four" href="default.asp" target="_blank">This
link changes font-family</a></b></p>
<p><b><a class="five" href="default.asp" target="_blank">This
link changes text-decoration</a></b></p>
</body>

</html>
```

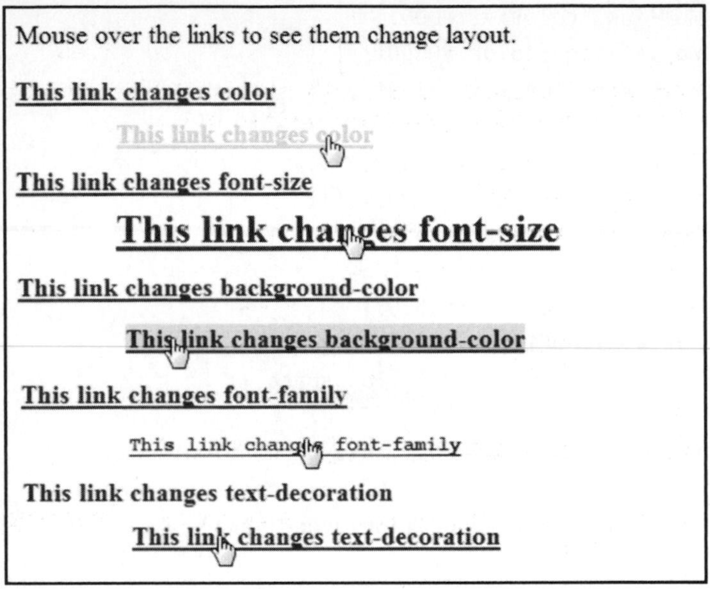

Mouse over the links to see them change layout.

<u>**This link changes color**</u>

<u>This link changes color</u>

<u>**This link changes font-size**</u>

<u>**This link changes font-size**</u>

<u>**This link changes background-color**</u>

<u>**This link changes background-color**</u>

<u>**This link changes font-family**</u>

<u>This link changes font-family</u>

This link changes text-decoration

This link changes text-decoration

Figure 21.2

Pseudo-Classes and CSS Classes

Pseudo-classes can be combined with CSS classes:

```
a.red:visited {color:#FF0000}
<a class="red" href="css_syntax.asp">CSS Syntax</a>
```

If the link in the previous example has been visited, it will be displayed in red.

CSS—The :first-child Pseudo-Class

The :first-child pseudo-class matches a specified element that is the first child of another element.

> **NOTE** For :first-child to work in IE, a <!DOCTYPE> must be declared.

Match the First <p> Element

In the following example, the selector matches any <p> element that is the first child of any element. The results of the code are shown in Figure 21.3.

```
<!DOCTYPE HTML PUBLIC "-//W3C//DTD HTML 4.01 Transitional//
  EN" "http://www.w3.org/TR/html4/loose.dtd">
<head>
<style type="text/css">
  p:first-child {font-weight:bold}
</style>
</head>

<body>
<p>I am a strong man.</p>
<p>I am a strong man.</p>

<p><b>Note:</b> For :first-child to work in IE, a DOCTYPE
  must be declared.</p>
</body>
</html>
```

I am a strong man.

I am a strong man.

Note: For :first-child to work in IE, a DOCTYPE must be declared.

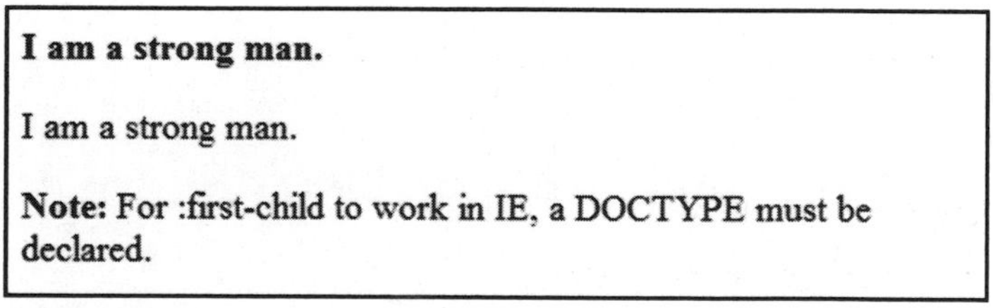

Figure 21.3

Match the First <i> Element in All <p> Elements

In the following example, the selector matches the first <i> element in all <p> elements. The results are shown in Figure 21.4.

```
<!DOCTYPE HTML PUBLIC "-//W3C//DTD HTML 4.01 Transitional//
  EN" "http://www.w3.org/TR/html4/loose.dtd">
<html>
<head>
<style type="text/css">
  p > i:first-child {font-weight:bold}
```

(continued)

203

(continued)

```
    </style>
    </head>

    <body>
    <p>I am a <i>strong</i> man. I am a <i>strong</i> man.</p>
    <p>I am a <i>strong</i> man. I am a <i>strong</i> man.</p>
    <p><b>Note:</b> For :first-child to work in IE, a DOCTYPE
       must be declared.</p>
    </body>
    </html>
```

I am a ***strong*** man. I am a *strong* man.

I am a ***strong*** man. I am a *strong* man.

Note: For :first-child to work in IE, a DOCTYPE must be declared.

Figure 21.4

Match All <i> Elements in All First Child <p> Elements

In the following example, the selector matches all **<i>** elements in **<p>** elements that are the first child of another element. The results are shown in Figure 21.5.

Try it yourself >>

```
<!DOCTYPE HTML PUBLIC "-//W3C//DTD HTML 4.01 Transitional//
    EN" "http://www.w3.org/TR/html4/loose.dtd">
<html>
<head>
<style type="text/css">
  p:first-child i {font-weight:bold}
</style>
</head>

<body>
<p>I am a <i>strong</i> man. I am a <i>strong</i> man.</p>
<p>I am a <i>strong</i> man. I am a <i>strong</i> man.</p>
```

```
<p><b>Note:</b> For :first-child to work in IE, a DOCTYPE
   must be declared.</p>
</body>
</html>
```

I am a *strong* man. I am a *strong* man.

I am a *strong* man. I am a *strong* man.

Note: For :first-child to work in IE, a DOCTYPE must be declared.

Figure 21.5

CSS—The :lang Pseudo-Class

The :lang pseudo-class allows you to define special rules for different languages.

> **NOTE** Internet Explorer 8 (and higher) supports the :lang pseudo-class if a
> <!DOCTYPE> is specified.

In the following example, the :lang class defines the marks that will surround a quotation for q elements with lang="no". The results are shown in Figure 21.6.

Try it yourself >>

```
<!DOCTYPE HTML PUBLIC "-//W3C//DTD HTML 4.01 Transitional//
   EN" "http://www.w3.org/TR/html4/loose.dtd">
<html>
<head>
<style type="text/css">
   q:lang(no) {quotes: "~" "~";}
</style>
</head>

<body>
<p>Some text <q lang="no">A quote in a paragraph</q> Some
   text.</p>
<p>In this example, :lang defines the quotation marks for q
   elements with lang="no":</p>
```

(continued)

(continued)

```
<p><b>Note:</b> Internet Explorer 8 (and higher) supports
   the :lang pseudo class if a !DOCTYPE is specified.</p>
</body>
</html>
```

> Some text ~A quote in a paragraph~ Some text.
>
> In this example, :lang defines the quotation marks for q elements
> with lang="no":
>
> **Note:** Internet Explorer 8 (and higher) supports the :lang pseudo
> class if a !DOCTYPE is specified.

Figure 21.6

The :focus Pseudo-Class

Use the :focus pseudo-class to highlight a selected input field, as shown in
Figure 21.7.

Try it yourself >>

```
<!DOCTYPE html PUBLIC "-//W3C//DTD XHTML 1.0 Transitional//
   EN" "http://www.w3.org/TR/xhtml1/DTD/xhtml1-transitional.
   dtd">
<html>
<head>
<style type="text/css">
  input:focus {background-color:yellow;}
</style>
</head>

<body>
<form action="form_action.asp" method="get">
First name: <input type="text" name="fname" /><br />
Last name: <input type="text" name="lname" /><br />
<input type="submit" value="Submit" />
</form>

<p><b>Note:</b> Internet Explorer 8 (and higher) supports
   the :focus pseudo-class if a !DOCTYPE is specified.</p>
```

```
</body>
</html>
```

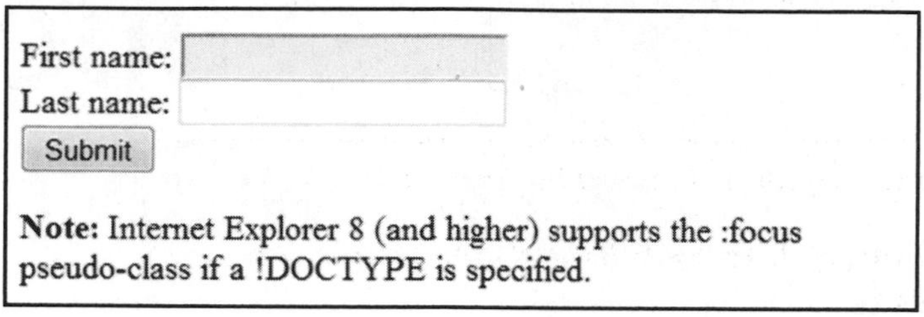

First name: [   ]

Last name: [   ]

[Submit]

Note: Internet Explorer 8 (and higher) supports the :focus pseudo-class if a !DOCTYPE is specified.

Figure 21.7

Pseudo-Classes

The CSS column indicates in which CSS version the property is defined (CSS1 or CSS2).

Pseudo name	Description	CSS
:active	Adds a style to an element that is activated	1
:first-child	Adds a style to an element that is the first child of another element	2
:focus	Adds a style to an element that has keyboard input focus	2
Pseudo name	Description	CSS
:hover	Adds a style to an element when you mouse over it	1
:lang	Adds a style to an element with a specific lang attribute	2
:link	Adds a style to an unvisited link	1
:visited	Adds a style to a visited link	1

CHAPTER 22

CSS PSEUDO-ELEMENTS

CSS pseudo-elements are used to add special effects to some selectors.

Syntax

The syntax of pseudo-elements:

```
selector:pseudo-element {property:value}
```

CSS classes can also be used with pseudo-elements:

```
selector.class:pseudo-element {property:value}
```

The :first-line Pseudo-Element

The :first-line pseudo-element is used to add a special style to the first line of text.

In the following example the browser formats the first line of text in a **p** element according to the style in the :first-line pseudo-element (where the browser breaks the line depends on the size of the browser window). The results are shown in Figure 22.1.

```
p:first-line
{
  color:#ff0000;
  font-variant:small-caps;
}
```

Try it yourself >>

```
<html>
<head>
<style type="text/css">
```

```
        p:first-line
        {
          color:#ff0000;
          font-variant:small-caps;
        }
    </style>
    </head>

    <body>
    <p>You can use the :first-line pseudo-element to add a
        special effect to the first line of a text.</p>
    </body>
    </html>
```

YOU CAN USE THE :FIRST-LINE PSEUDO-ELEMENT TO ADD A
special effect to the first line of a text.

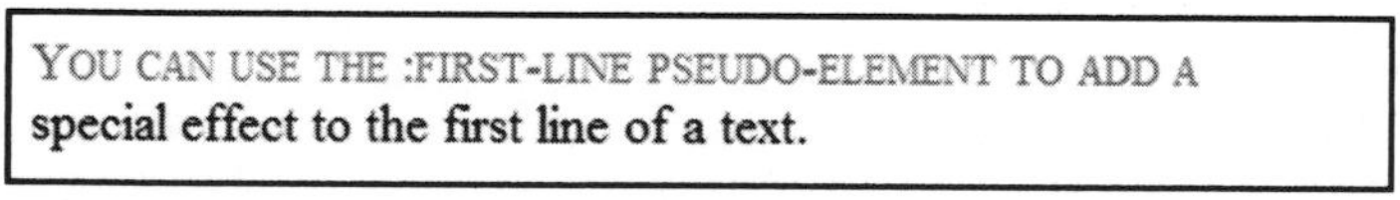

Figure 22.1

NOTE The :first-line pseudo-element can only be used with block-level elements.

:first-line PSEUDO-ELEMENT PROPERTIES

The following properties apply to the :first-line pseudo-element:

▶▶ font properties

▶▶ color properties

▶▶ background properties

▶▶ word-spacing

▶▶ letter-spacing

▶▶ text-decoration

▶▶ vertical-align

▶▶ text-transform

▶▶ line-height

▶▶ clear

209

The :first-letter Pseudo-Element

The :first-letter pseudo-element is used to add a special style to the first letter of text. The results are shown in Figure 22.2.

```
p:first-letter
{
    color:#ff0000;
    font-size:xx-large;
}
```

NOTE The :first-letter pseudo-element can only be used with block-level elements.

Try it yourself >>

```
<html>
<head>
<style type="text/css">
  p:first-letter
  {
    color:#ff0000;
    font-size:xx-large;
  }
</style>
</head>

<body>
<p>You can use the :first-letter pseudo-element to add a
   special effect to the first character of a text!</p>
</body>
</html>
```

Y ou can use the :first-letter pseudo-element to add a special effect to the first character of a text!

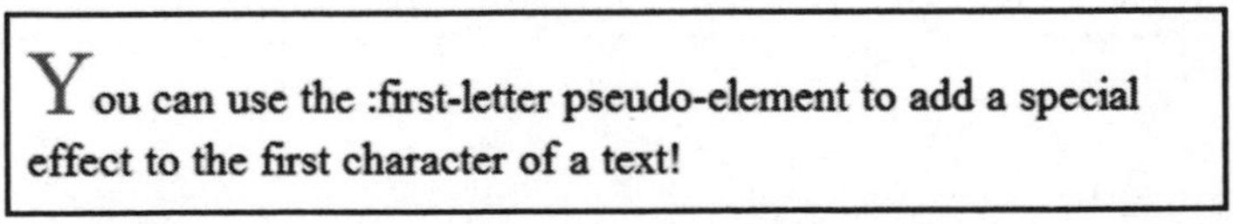

Figure 22.2

:first-letter PSEUDO-ELEMENT PROPERTIES

The following properties apply to the `:first-letter` pseudo-element:

- font properties
- color properties
- background properties
- margin properties
- padding properties
- border properties

- text-decoration
- vertical-align (only if **float** is **none**)
- text-transform
- line-height
- float
- clear

Pseudo-Elements and CSS Classes

Pseudo-elements can be combined with CSS classes:

```
p.article:first-letter {color:#ff0000}
<p class="article">A paragraph in an article</p>
```

This example will display the first letter of all paragraphs with `class="article"` in red.

Multiple Pseudo-Elements

Several pseudo-elements can also be combined.

In the following example, the first letter of a paragraph will be red in an xx-large font size. The rest of the first line will be blue and in small-caps. The rest of the paragraph will be the default font size and color. The results are shown in Figure 22.3.

```
p:first-letter
{
  color:#ff0000;
  font-size:xx-large;
}
p:first-line
{
  color:#0000ff;
  font-variant:small-caps;
}
```

Try it yourself >>

```
<html>
<head>
<style type="text/css">
  p:first-letter
  {
    color:#ff0000;
    font-size:xx-large;
  }
  p:first-line
  {
    color:#0000ff;
    font-variant:small-caps;
  }
</style>
</head>

<body>
<p>You can combine the :first-letter and :first-line pseudo-
   elements to add a special effect to the first letter and
   the first line of a text!</p>
</body>
</html>
```

> YOU CAN COMBINE THE :FIRST-LETTER AND :FIRST-LINE PSEUDO-elements to add a special effect to the first letter and the first line of a text!

Figure 22.3

The :before Pseudo-Element

The `:before` pseudo-element can be used to insert some content before the content of an element.

The following example inserts an image before each `<h1>` element. The results are shown in Figure 22.4.

```
h1:before
{
  content:url(smiley.gif);
}
```

Try it yourself >>

```
<!DOCTYPE html PUBLIC "-//W3C//DTD XHTML 1.0 Transitional//
  EN" "http://www.w3.org/TR/xhtml1/DTD/xhtml1-transitional.
  dtd">
<html>
<head>
<style type="text/css">
  h1:before {content:url(smiley.gif);}
</style>
</head>

<body>
<h1>This is a Heading</h1>
<p>The :before pseudo-element inserts content before an
  element.</p>
<h1>This is a Heading</h1>
<p><b>Note:</b> Internet Explorer 8 (and higher) supports
  the content property if a !DOCTYPE is specified.</p>
</body>
</html>
```

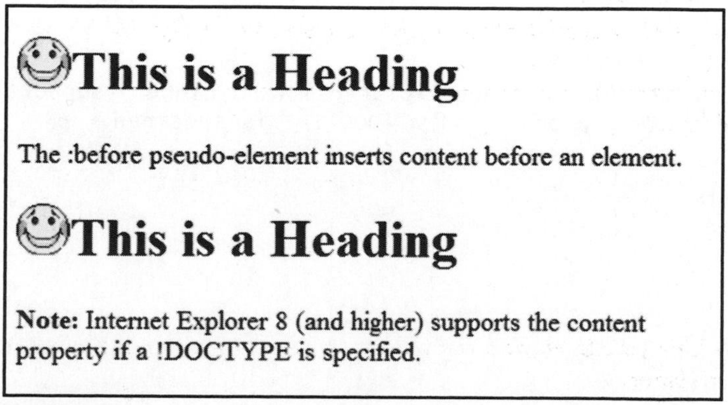

Figure 22.4

213

The :after Pseudo-Element

The :after pseudo-element can be used to insert some content after the content of an element.

The following example inserts an image after each <h1> element. The results are shown in Figure 22.5.

```
h1:after
{
  content:url(smiley.gif);
}
```

Try it yourself >>

```
<!DOCTYPE html PUBLIC "-//W3C//DTD XHTML 1.0 Transitional//
  EN" "http://www.w3.org/TR/xhtml1/DTD/xhtml1-transitional.
  dtd">
<html>
<head>
<style type="text/css">
  h1:after {content:url(smiley.gif);}
</style>
</head>

<body>
<h1>This is a Heading</h1>
<p>The :after pseudo-element inserts content after an
  element.</p>
<h1>This is a Heading</h1>
<p><b>Note:</b> Internet Explorer 8 (and higher) supports
  the content property if a !DOCTYPE is specified.</p>
</body>
</html>
```

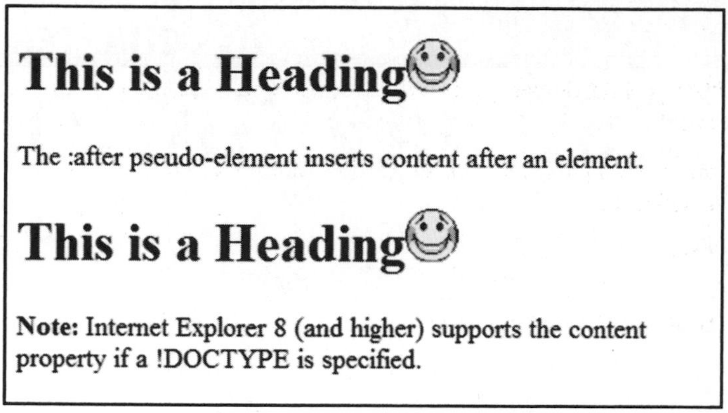

This is a Heading😊

The :after pseudo-element inserts content after an element.

This is a Heading😊

Note: Internet Explorer 8 (and higher) supports the content property if a !DOCTYPE is specified.

Figure 22.5

Pseudo-Elements

The CSS column indicates in which CSS version the property is defined (CSS1 or CSS2).

Pseudo name	Description	CSS
:after	Adds content after an element	2
:before	Adds content before an element	2
:first-letter	Adds a style to the first character of a text	1
:first-line	Adds a style to the first line of a text	1

CHAPTER 23

CSS NAVIGATION BAR

Demo: Navigation Bar

HOME   NEWS   ARTICLES   FORUM   CONTACT   ABOUT

Navigation Bars

Easy-to-use navigation is important for any Web site.

With CSS, you can transform boring HTML menus into good-looking navigation bars.

Navigation Bar = List of Links

A navigation bar needs standard HTML as a base.

In our examples, we build the navigation bar from a standard HTML list.

A navigation bar is basically a list of links, as shown in Figure 23.1, so using the <ul> and <li> elements makes perfect sense:

Try it yourself >>

```
<html>
<body>
<ul>
  <li><a href="home">Home</a></li>
  <li><a href="news">News</a></li>
  <li><a href="contact">Contact</a></li>
  <li><a href="about">About</a></li>
</ul>

</body>
</html>
```

- Home
- News
- Contact
- About

Figure 23.1

Now let's remove the bullets and the margins and padding from the list. Figure 23.2 shows this result.

Try it yourself >>

```html
<html>
<head>
<style>
  ul
  {
    list-style-type:none;
    margin:0;
    padding:0;
  }
</style>
</head>
<body>
<ul>
  <li><a href="home">Home</a></li>
  <li><a href="news">News</a></li>
  <li><a href="contact">Contact</a></li>
  <li><a href="about">About</a></li>
</ul>
</body>
</html>
```

Home
News
Contact
About

Figure 23.2

Example explained:

▸▸ `list-style-type:none`—Removes the bullets. A navigation bar does not need list markers.

▸▸ Setting margins and padding to 0 removes browser default settings.

The code in the previous example is the standard code used in both vertical and horizontal navigation bars.

Vertical Navigation Bar

To build a vertical navigation bar, we only need to style the <a> elements in addition to the previous code. The result is shown in Figure 23.3.

```
a
{
    display:block;
    width:60px;
}
```

Example explained:

▸▸ `display:block`—Displaying the links as block elements makes the whole link area clickable (not just the text), and it allows us to specify the width.

▸▸ `width:60px`—Block elements take up the full width available by default. We want to specify a 60 px width.

Try it yourself >>

```
<html>
<head>
<style type="text/css">
  ul
  {
    list-style-type:none;
    margin:0;
    padding:0;
  }
  a
  {
    display:block;
    width:60px;
    background-color:#dddddd;
  }
```

```
</style>
</head>

<body>
<ul>
  <li><a href="home">Home</a></li>
  <li><a href="news">News</a></li>
  <li><a href="contact">Contact</a></li>
  <li><a href="about">About</a></li>
</ul>

<p>A background color is added to the links to show the link
  area.</p>
<p>Notice that the whole link area is clickable, not just
  the text.</p>
</body>
</html>
```

Figure 23.3

NOTE Always specify the width for <a> elements in a vertical navigation bar. If you omit the width, IE6 can produce unexpected results.

Fully Styled Vertical Navigation Bar

Here is the code for an example of a fully styled vertical navigation bar, as shown in Figure 23.4.

Try it yourself >>

```
<html>
<head>
<style type="text/css">
   ul
   {
     list-style-type:none;
     margin:0;
     padding:0;
   }
   a:link,a:visited
   {
      display:block;
      font-weight:bold;
      color:#FFFFFF;
      background-color:#98bf21;
      width:120px;
      text-align:center;
      padding:4px;
      text-decoration:none;
      text-transform:uppercase;
   }
   a:hover,a:active
   {
      background-color:#7A991A;
   }
</style>
</head>

<body>
<ul>
   <li><a href="home">Home</a></li>
   <li><a href="news">News</a></li>
   <li><a href="contact">Contact</a></li>
   <li><a href="about">About</a></li>
</ul>
</body>
</html>
```

220

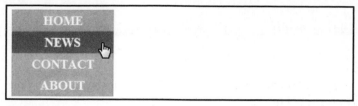

Figure 23.4

Horizontal Navigation Bar

There are two ways to create a horizontal navigation bar: use *inline* or *floating* list items.

Both methods work fine, but if you want the links to be the same size, you have to use the floating method.

Inline List Items

One way to build a horizontal navigation bar is to specify the `<li>` elements as inline, in addition to the "standard" code we used for the vertical navigation bar. The result of this is shown in Figure 23.5.

```
li
{
   display:inline;
}
```

Example explained:

▸ `display:inline;`—By default, `<li>` elements are block elements. Here, we remove the line breaks before and after each list item, to display them on one line.

Try it yourself >>

```
<html>
<head>
<style type="text/css">
  ul
  {
    list-style-type:none;
    margin:0;
```

(continued)

221

(continued)

```
      padding:0;
    }
    li
    {
      display:inline;
    }
  </style>
  </head>

  <body>
  <ul>
    <li><a href="home">Home</a></li>
    <li><a href="news">News</a></li>
    <li><a href="contact">Contact</a></li>
    <li><a href="about">About</a></li>
  </ul>

  </body>
  </html>
```

Home News Contact About

Figure 23.5

Fully Styled Inline Horizontal Navigation Bar

Here is the code for an example of a fully styled horizontal navigation bar created using the inline method. The results are shown in Figure 23.6.

```
  <html>
  <head>
  <style type="text/css">
    ul
    {
      list-style-type:none;
```

```
    margin:0;
    padding:0;
    padding-top:6px;
    padding-bottom:6px;
  }
  li
  {
    display:inline;
  }
  a:link,a:visited
  {
    font-weight:bold;
    color:#FFFFFF;
    background-color:#98bf21;
    text-align:center;
    padding:6px;
    text-decoration:none;
    text-transform:uppercase;
  }
  a:hover,a:active
  {
    background-color:#7A991A;
  }
</style>
</head>

<body>
<ul>
  <li><a href="home">Home</a></li>
  <li><a href="news">News</a></li>
  <li><a href="contact">Contact</a></li>
  <li><a href="about">About</a></li>
</ul>

<p><b>Note:</b> If you only set the padding for a elements
  (and not ul), the links will go outside the ul element.
  Therefore, we have added a top and bottom padding for the
  ul element.</p>
</body>
</html>
```

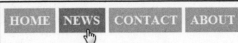

HOME
NEWS
CONTACT
ABOUT
Note: If you only set the padding for a elements (and not ul), the links will go outside the ul element. Therefore, we have added a top and bottom padding for the ul element.

Figure 23.6

Floating List Items

In the previous example the links have different widths.

For all the links to have an equal width, float the `<li>` elements and specify a width for the <a> elements. The result of this code is shown in Figure 23.7.

```
li
{
  float:left;
}
a
{
  display:block;
  width:60px;
}
```

Example explained:

- `float:left`—Use float to get block elements to slide next to each other.
- `display:block`—Displaying the links as block elements makes the whole link area clickable (not just the text), and it allows us to specify the width.
- `width:60px`—Because block elements take up the full width available, they cannot float next to each other. We specify the width of the links to **60px**.

Try it yourself >>

```
<!DOCTYPE html PUBLIC "-//W3C//DTD XHTML 1.0 Transitional//
  EN" "http://www.w3.org/TR/xhtml1/DTD/xhtml1-transitional.
  dtd">
<html>
<head>
<style type="text/css">
  ul
  {
```

```
    list-style-type:none;
    margin:0;
    padding:0;
    overflow:hidden;
  }
  li
  {
    float:left;
  }
  a
  {
    display:block;
    width:60px;
    background-color:#dddddd;
  }
</style>
</head>

<body>
<ul>
  <li><a href="home">Home</a></li>
  <li><a href="news">News</a></li>
  <li><a href="contact">Contact</a></li>
  <li><a href="about">About</a></li>
</ul>

<p><b>Note:</b> If a !DOCTYPE is not specified, floating items
  can produce unexpected results.</p>

<p>A background color is added to the links to show the
  link area. The whole link area is clickable, not just the
  text.</p>

<p><b>Note:</b> overflow:hidden is added to the ul element to
  prevent li elements from going outside of the list.</p>

</body>
</html>
```

225

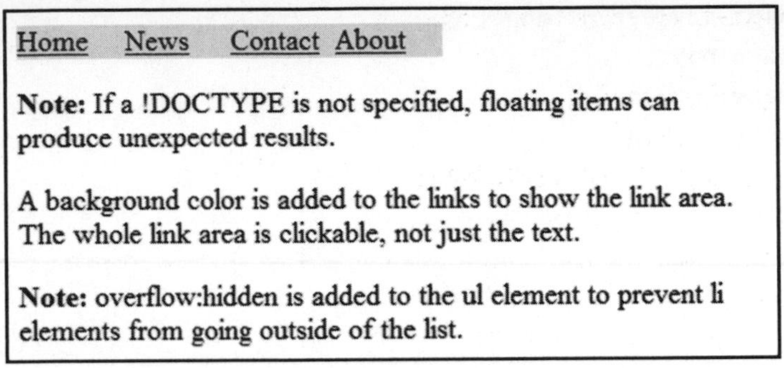

Home   News   Contact About

Note: If a !DOCTYPE is not specified, floating items can produce unexpected results.

A background color is added to the links to show the link area. The whole link area is clickable, not just the text.

Note: overflow:hidden is added to the ul element to prevent li elements from going outside of the list.

Figure 23.7

Fully Styled Floating Horizontal Navigation Bar

Here is the code for an example of a fully styled horizontal navigation bar created using the float method. The results are shown in Figure 23.8.

```
<html>
<head>
<style type="text/css">
  ul
  {
    list-style-type:none;
    margin:0;
    padding:0;
    overflow:hidden;
  }
  li
  {
    float:left;
  }
  a:link,a:visited
  {
    display:block;
    width:120px;
    font-weight:bold;
    color:#FFFFFF;
    background-color:#98bf21;
    text-align:center;
    padding:4px;
    text-decoration:none;
```

```
    text-transform:uppercase;
  }
  a:hover,a:active
  {
    background-color:#7A991A;
  }
</style>
</head>

<body>
<ul>
  <li><a href="home">Home</a></li>
  <li><a href="news">News</a></li>
  <li><a href="contact">Contact</a></li>
  <li><a href="about">About</a></li>
</ul>
</body>
</html>
```

Figure 23.8

CHAPTER 24

CSS IMAGE GALLERY

CSS can be used to create an image gallery, as shown in Figure 24.1.

```html
<html>
<head>
<style type="text/css">
  div.img
  {
    margin:2px;
    border:1px solid #0000ff;
    height:auto;
    width:auto;
    float:left;
    text-align:center;
  }
  div.img img
  {
    display:inline;
    margin:3px;
    border:1px solid #ffffff;
  }
  div.img a:hover img
  {
    border:1px solid #0000ff;
  }
  div.desc
  {
    text-align:center;
    font-weight:normal;
```

```
        width:120px;
        margin:2px;
    }
</style>
</head>
<body>


<div class="img">
   <a target="_blank" href="klematis_big.htm">
   <img src="klematis_small.jpg" alt="Klematis" width="110"
      height="90" />
   </a>
   <div class="desc">Add a description of the image here
      </div>
</div>
<div class="img">
   <a target="_blank" href="klematis2_big.htm">
   <img src="klematis2_small.jpg" alt="Klematis" width="110"
      height="90" />
   </a>
   <div class="desc">Add a description of the image here
      </div>
</div>
<div class="img">
   <a target="_blank" href="klematis3_big.htm">
   <img src="klematis3_small.jpg" alt="Klematis" width="110"
      height="90" />
   </a>
   <div class="desc">Add a description of the image here
      </div>
</div>
<div class="img">
   <a target="_blank" href="klematis4_big.htm">
   <img src="klematis4_small.jpg" alt="Klematis" width="110"
      height="90" />
   </a>
   <div class="desc">Add a description of the image here
      </div>
</div>
```

(continued)

229

(continued)

```
        </body>
        </html>
```

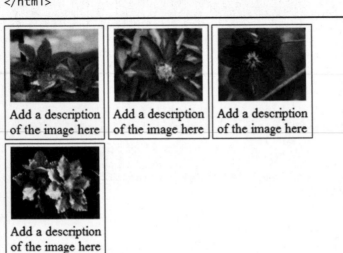

Figure 24.1

CHAPTER 25

CSS IMAGE OPACITY / TRANSPARENCY

Creating transparent images with CSS is easy.

> **NOTE** This is not yet a CSS standard. However, it works in all modern browsers and is a part of the W3C CSS 3 recommendation.

Creating a Transparent Image

First we show you how to create a transparent image with CSS.

Figure 25.1 is a regular image:

Figure 25.1

Figure 25.2 shows the same image with transparency:

Figure 25.2

Look at the following source code:

```
<img src="klematis.jpg" width="150" height="113" alt=
  "klematis" style="opacity:0.4;filter:alpha(opacity=40)" />
```

Firefox uses the property `opacity:x` for transparency, while IE uses `filter:alpha(opacity=x)`.

In Firefox (`opacity:x`), *x* can be a value from 0.0–1.0. A lower value makes the element more transparent.

TIP The CSS3 syntax for transparency is `opacity:x`.

In IE (`filter:alpha(opacity=x)`), *x* can be a value from 0–100. A lower value makes the element more transparent.

Image Transparency—Mouseover Effect

You can set a mouseover effect so that when you mouseover the images, they stop being transparent and return to being opaque, as shown in Figure 25.3.

Figure 25.3

The source code looks like this:

```
<img src="klematis.jpg" style="opacity:0.4;filter:alpha
  (opacity=40)"
  onmouseover="this.style.opacity=1;this.filters.alpha.
  opacity=100"
  onmouseout="this.style.opacity=0.4;this.filters.alpha.
  opacity=40" />

<img src="klematis2.jpg" style="opacity:0.4;filter:alpha
  (opacity=40)"
  onmouseover="this.style.opacity=1;this.filters.alpha.
  opacity=100"
  onmouseout="this.style.opacity=0.4;this.filters.alpha.
  opacity=40" />
```

We see that the first line of the source code is similar to the source code in the first example. In addition, we have added an onmouseover attribute and an onmouseout attribute. The onmouseover attribute defines what will happen when the mouse pointer moves over the image. In this case, we want the image to *not* be transparent when we move the mouse pointer over it.

The syntax for this in Firefox is this.style.opacity=1, and the syntax in IE is this.filters.alpha.opacity=100.

When the mouse pointer moves away from the image, we want the image to be transparent again. This is done in the onmouseout attribute.

Here is all the code for creating a page with these two images:

```
<html>
<head>
<style type="text/css">
  img
  {
```

(continued)

233

(continued)

```
        opacity:0.4;
        filter:alpha(opacity=40);
    }
</style>
</head>
<body>

<h1>Image Transparency</h1>
<img src="klematis.jpg" width="150" height="113"
  alt="klematis"
  onmouseover="this.style.opacity=1;this.filters.alpha.
  opacity=100"
  onmouseout="this.style.opacity=0.4;this.filters.alpha.
  opacity=40" />

<img src="klematis2.jpg" width="150" height="113"
  alt="klematis"
  onmouseover="this.style.opacity=1;this.filters.alpha.
  opacity=100"
  onmouseout="this.style.opacity=0.4;this.filters.alpha.
  opacity=40" />
</body>
</html>
```

Text in Transparent Box

You can also use transparency to layer text over a background of images, as shown in Figure 25.4.

Try it yourself >>

```
<html>
<head>
<style type="text/css">
div.background
{
  width:500px;
  height:250px;
  background:url(klematis.jpg) repeat;
  border:2px solid black;
}
```

```
div.transbox
{
  width:400px;
  height:180px;
  margin:30px 50px;
  background-color:#ffffff;
  border:1px solid black;
  /* for IE */
  filter:alpha(opacity=60);
  /* CSS3 standard */
  opacity:0.6;
}
div.transbox p
{
  margin:30px 40px;
  font-weight:bold;
  color:#000000;
}
</style>
</head>

<body>

<div class="background">
<div class="transbox">
<p>This is some text that is placed in the transparent box.
   This is some text that is placed in the transparent box.
   This is some text that is placed in the transparent box.
   This is some text that is placed in the transparent box.
   This is some text that is placed in the transparent box.
</p>
</div>
</div>

</body>
</html>
```

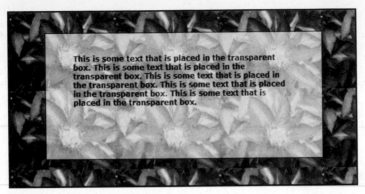

Figure 25.4

First, we create a div element (class="background") with a fixed height and width, a background image, and a border. Then we create a smaller div (class="transbox") inside the first div element. This div also has a fixed width, a background image, and a border. In addition we make this div transparent.

Inside the transparent div, we add some text inside a p element.

CHAPTER 26

CSS IMAGE SPRITES

An image sprite is a collection of images put into a single image.

A Web page with many images can take a long time to load and generates multiple server requests.

Using image sprites reduces the number of server requests and saves bandwidth.

Simple Example

Instead of using three separate images, we use this single image (img_navsprites. gif), shown in Figure 26.1.

With CSS, we can show just the part of the image we need.

In the following example, the CSS specifies which part of the img_navsprites.gif image to show. The results of the code are shown in Figure 26.2.

Figure 26.1

```
img.home
{
  width:46px;
  height:44px;
  background:url(img_navsprites.gif) 0 0;
}
```

Try it yourself >>

```
<!DOCTYPE html PUBLIC "-//W3C//DTD XHTML 1.0 Strict//EN"
    "http://www.w3.org/TR/xhtml1/DTD/xhtml1-strict.dtd">
<html>
<head>
```

(continued)

(continued)

```
<style type="text/css">
  img.home
  {
    width:46px;
    height:44px;
    background:url(img_navsprites.gif) 0 0;
  }
  img.next
  {
    width:43px;
    height:44px;
    background:url(img_navsprites.gif) -91px 0;
  }
</style>
</head>

<body>
<img class="home" src="img_trans.gif" width="1" height="1"
   />
<br /><br />
<img class="next" src="img_trans.gif" width="1" height="1"
   />
</body>
</html>
```

Figure 26.2

Example Explained

▸▸ `<img class="home" src="img_trans.gif" />`—Only defines a small
transparent image because the src attribute cannot be empty. The displayed
image will be the background image we specify in CSS.

▸▸ `width:46px;height:44px;`—Defines the portion of the image we want to use.

▸▸ `background:url(img_navsprites.gif) 0 0;`—Defines the background image and its position (left 0px, top 0px).

This is the easiest way to use image sprites; now we want to expand it by using links and hover effects.

Create a Navigation List

We want to use the sprite image (img_navsprites.gif) to create a navigation list.

We will use an HTML list, because it can be a link and also supports a background image.

```
#navlist{position:relative;}
#navlist li{margin:0;padding:0;list-style:none;
    position:absolute;top:0;}
#navlist li, #navlist a{height:44px;display:block;}

#home{left:0px;width:46px;}
#home{background:url('img_navsprites.gif') 0 0;}

#prev{left:63px;width:43px;}
#prev{background:url('img_navsprites.gif') -47px 0;}

#next{left:129px;width:43px;}
#next{background:url('img_navsprites.gif') -91px 0;}
```

Example Explained

▸▸ `#navlist{position:relative;}`—Position is set to relative to allow absolute positioning inside it.

▸▸ `#navlist li{margin:0;padding:0;list-style:none;` `position:absolute;top:0;}`—Margin and padding are set to 0, list-style is removed, and all list items are absolute positioned.

▸▸ `#navlist li, #navlist a{height:44px;display:block;}`—The height of all the images is 44px.

Now start to position and style each specific part:

▸▸ `#home{left:0px;width:46px;}`—Positioned all the way to the left and sets the width of the image to 46px.

▸ `#home{background:url(img_navsprites.gif) 0 0;}`—Defines the background image and its position (left 0px, top 0px).

▸ `#prev{left:63px;width:43px;}`—Positioned 63px to the right (#home width 46px + some extra space between items) and sets the width to 43px.

▸ `#prev{background:url('img_navsprites.gif') -47px 0;}`—Defines the background image 47px to the right (#home width 46px + 1px line divider).

▸ `#next{left:129px;width:43px;}`— Positioned 129px to the right (start of #prev is 63px + #prev width 43px + extra space) and sets the width to 43px.

▸ `#next{background:url('img_navsprites.gif') no-repeat -91px 0;}`—Defines the background image 91px to the right (#home width 46px + 1px line divider + #prev width 43px + 1px line divider).

Figure 26.3 shows the result of this code.

Try it yourself >>

```
<!DOCTYPE html PUBLIC "-//W3C//DTD XHTML 1.0 Strict//EN"
  "http://www.w3.org/TR/xhtml1/DTD/xhtml1-strict.dtd">
<html>
<head>
<style type="text/css">
  #navlist{position:relative;}
  #navlist li{margin:0;padding:0;list-style:none;
    position:absolute;top:0;}
  #navlist li, #navlist a{height:44px;display:block;}

  #home{left:0px;width:46px;}
  #home{background:url('img_navsprites.gif') 0 0;}

  #prev{left:63px;width:43px;}
  #prev{background:url('img_navsprites.gif') -47px 0;}

  #next{left:129px;width:43px;}
  #next{background:url('img_navsprites.gif') -91px 0;}
</style>
</head>

<body>
<ul id="navlist">
  <li id="home"><a href="default.asp"></a></li>
```

```
     <li id="prev"><a href="css_intro.asp"></a></li>
     <li id="next"><a href="css_syntax.asp"></a></li>
</ul>
</body>
</html>
```

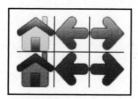

Figure 26.3

Hover Effect

Now we want to add a hover effect to our navigation list.

Our new image (img_navsprites_hover.gif), shown in Figure 26.4, contains three navigation images and three images to use for hover effects.

Because this is one single image, and not six separate files, there will be **no loading delay** when a user hovers over the image.

We add only three lines of code to add the hover effect. Figure 26.5 shows the results of this code.

```
#home a:hover{background: url('img_navsprites_hover.gif')
   0 -45px;}

#prev a:hover{background: url('img_navsprites_hover.gif')
   -47px -45px;}

#next a:hover{background: url('img_navsprites_hover.gif')
   -91px -45px;}
```

Figure 26.4

Example explained:

▸ Because the list item contains a link, we can use the `:hover` pseudo-class.

▸ `#home a:hover{background: transparent url(img_navsprites_hover.gif) 0 -45px;}`—For all three hover images we specify the same background position, only 45px farther down.

```
<!DOCTYPE html PUBLIC "-//W3C//DTD XHTML 1.0 Strict//EN"
   "http://www.w3.org/TR/xhtml1/DTD/xhtml1-strict.dtd">
<html>
<head>
<style type="text/css">
   #navlist{position:relative;}
   #navlist li{margin:0;padding:0;list-style:none;
     position:absolute;top:0;}
   #navlist li, #navlist a{height:44px;display:block;}

   #home{left:0px;width:46px;}
   #home{background:url('img_navsprites_hover.gif') 0 0;}
   #home a:hover{background: url('img_navsprites_hover.gif')
     0 -45px;}

   #prev{left:63px;width:43px;}
   #prev{background:url('img_navsprites_hover.gif') -47px
     0;}
   #prev a:hover{background: url('img_navsprites_hover.gif')
     -47px -45px;}

   #next{left:129px;width:43px;}
   #next{background:url('img_navsprites_hover.gif') -91px
     0;}
   #next a:hover{background: url('img_navsprites_hover.gif')
     -91px -45px;}
</style>
</head>

<body>
<ul id="navlist">
   <li id="home"><a href="default.asp"></a></li>
```

(continued)

```
    <li id="prev"><a href="css_intro.asp"></a></li>
    <li id="next"><a href="css_syntax.asp"></a></li>
</ul>
</body>
</html>
```

Figure 26.5

CHAPTER 27

CSS MEDIA TYPES

Media types allow you to specify how documents are presented in different media. The document can be displayed differently on the screen, on the paper, with an aural browser, and so on.

Media Types

Some CSS properties are designed only for a certain media. For example, the voice-family property is designed for aural user agents. Some other properties can be used for different media types. For example, the font-size property can be used for both screen and print media, but perhaps with different values. A document usually needs a larger font-size on a screen than on paper, and sans serif fonts are easier to read on the screen, while serif fonts are easier to read on paper.

The @media Rule

The @media rule allows different style rules for different media in the same style sheet.

The style in the example that follows tells the browser to display a 14 pixels Verdana font on the screen. But if the page is printed, it will be in a 10 pixels Times font. Notice that the font-weight is set to bold, both on screen and on paper:

```
<html>
<head>
<style>
  @media screen
  {
    p.test {font-family:verdana,sans-serif;font-size:14px}
  }
  @media print
  {
    p.test {font-family:times,serif;font-size:10px}
  }
```

```
@media screen,print
{
  p.test {font-weight:bold}
}
</style>
</head>

<body>
....
</body>
</html>
```

 See it yourself! Visit the w3schools page for this chapter (www.w3schools. com/css/css_mediatypes.asp) using Mozilla Firefox or IE 5+ and print the page. You will see that the paragraph under "Media Types" is displayed in another font and has a smaller font-size than the rest of the text.

Different Media Types

Note: The media type names are not case sensitive.

Media Type	Description
all	Used for all media type devices
aural	Used for speech and sound synthesizers
braille	Used for braille tactile feedback devices
embossed	Used for paged braille printers
handheld	Used for small or handheld devices
print	Used for printers
projection	Used for projected presentations, like slides
screen	Used for computer screens
tty	Used for media using a fixed-pitch character grid, like teletypes and terminals
tv	Used for television-type devices

CHAPTER 28

CSS ATTRIBUTE SELECTORS

It is possible to style HTML elements that have specific attributes, not just class and ID.

NOTE Internet Explorer 7 (and higher) supports attribute selectors only if a !DOCTYPE is specified. Attribute selection is *not* supported in IE6 and lower.

Attribute Selector

The following example styles all elements with a `title` attribute. The results of this code are shown in Figure 28.1.

```
[title] {color:blue;}
```

Try it yourself >>

```
<!DOCTYPE html PUBLIC "-//W3C//DTD XHTML 1.0 Transitional//
    EN" "http://www.w3.org/TR/xhtml1/DTD/xhtml1-transitional.
    dtd">
<html>
<head>
<style type="text/css">
  [title] {color:blue;}
</style>
</head>

<body>
<h2>Will apply to:</h2>
  <h1 title="Hello world">Hello world</h1>
  <a title="w3schools" href="http://w3schools.com">
    w3schools</a>
<hr />
```

```
<h2>Will not apply to:</h2>
  <p>Hello!</p>
</body>
</html>
```

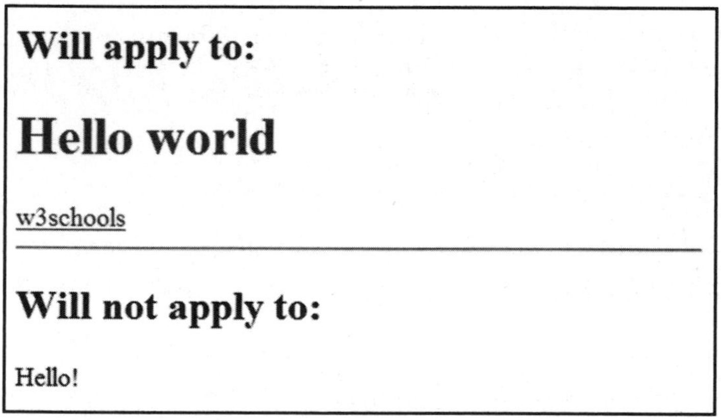

Will apply to:

Hello world

<u>w3schools</u>

Will not apply to:

Hello!

Figure 28.1

Attribute and Value Selector

The following example styles all elements with `title=w3schools`. The results of this code are shown in Figure 28.2.

```
[title=w3schools] {border:5px solid green;}
```

Try it yourself >>

```
<!DOCTYPE html PUBLIC "-//W3C//DTD XHTML 1.0 Transitional//
   EN" "http://www.w3.org/TR/xhtml1/DTD/xhtml1-transitional.
   dtd">
<html>
<head>
<style type="text/css">
  [title=w3schools] {border:5px solid green;}
</style>
</head>

<body>
<h2>Will apply to:</h2>
  <img title="w3schools" src="w3schools_logo.gif" width="270"
  height="50" />
```

(continued)

247

(continued)

```
<br />
  <a title="w3schools" href="http://w3schools.com">
    w3schools</a>
<hr />
<h2>Will not apply to:</h2>
  <p title="greeting">Hi!</p>
  <a class="w3schools" href="http://w3schools.com">
    w3schools</a>
</body>
</html>
```

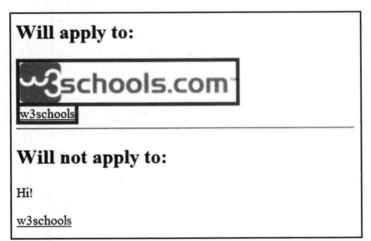

Figure 28.2

Attribute and Value Selector— Multiple Values

The following example styles all elements with a `title` attribute that contains a specified value. This works even if the attribute has space-separated values. The results of this code are shown in Figure 28.3.

```
[title~=hello] { color:blue; }
```

Try it yourself >>

```
<!DOCTYPE html PUBLIC "-//W3C//DTD XHTML 1.0 Transitional//
  EN" "http://www.w3.org/TR/xhtml1/DTD/xhtml1-transitional.
  dtd">
```

```
<html>
<head>
<style type="text/css">
  [title~=hello] {color:blue;}
</style>
</head>

<body>
<h2>Will apply to:</h2>
  <h1 title="hello world">Hello world</h1>
  <p title="student hello">Hello CSS students!</h1>
<hr />
<h2>Will not apply to:</h2>
  <p title="student">Hi CSS students!</p>
</body>
</html>
```

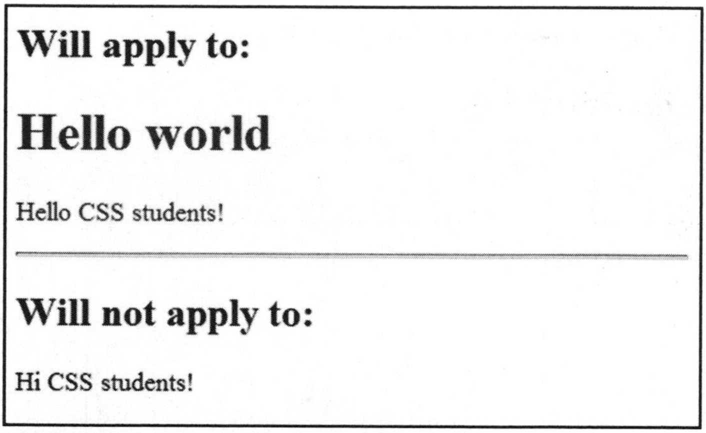

Will apply to:

Hello world

Hello CSS students!

Will not apply to:

Hi CSS students!

Figure 28.3

The following example styles all elements with a `lang` attribute that contains a specified value. This works even if the attribute has hyphen (-) separated values. The results of this code are shown in Figure 28.4.

```
[lang|=en] { color:blue; }
```

Try it yourself >>

```
<!DOCTYPE html PUBLIC "-//W3C//DTD XHTML 1.0 Transitional//
  EN" "http://www.w3.org/TR/xhtml1/DTD/xhtml1-transitional.
  dtd">
```

(continued)

(continued)

```html
<html>
<head>
<style type="text/css">
  [lang|=en]
  {
    color:blue;
  }
</style>
</head>

<body>
<h2>Will apply to:</h2>
  <p lang="en">Hello!</p>
  <p lang="en-us">Hi!</p>
  <p lang="en-gb">'Ello!</p>
<hr />
<h2>Will not apply to:</h2>
  <p lang="us">Hi!</p>
  <p lang="no">Hei!</p>
</body>
</html>
```

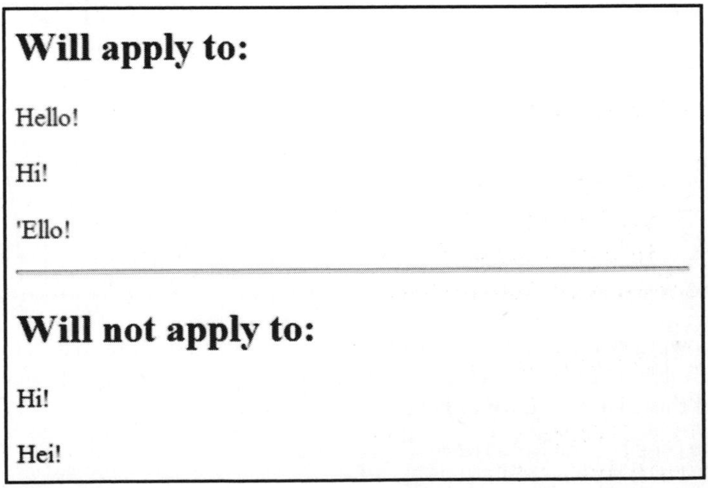

Will apply to:

Hello!

Hi!

'Ello!

___

Will not apply to:

Hi!

Hei!

Figure 28.4

Styling Forms

The attribute selectors are particularly useful for styling forms without class or ID. The results of this code are shown in Figure 28.5.

```
input[type="text"]
{
    width:150px;
    display:block;
    margin-bottom:10px;
    background-color:yellow;
}
input[type="button"]
{
    width:120px;
    margin-left:35px;
    display:block;
}
```

Try it yourself >>

```
<!DOCTYPE html PUBLIC "-//W3C//DTD XHTML 1.0 Transitional//
    EN" "http://www.w3.org/TR/xhtml1/DTD/xhtml1-transitional.
    dtd">
<html>
<head>
<style>
  input[type="text"]
  {
    width:150px;
    display:block;
    margin-bottom:10px;
    background-color:yellow;
  }
  input[type="button"]
  {
    width:120px;
    margin-left:35px;
    display:block;
  }
</style>
</head>
```

(continued)

(continued)

```
<body>

<form name="input" action="" method="get">
  Firstname:<input type="text" name="Name" value="Peter"
    size="20">
  Lastname:<input type="text" name="Name" value="Griffin"
    size="20">
  <input type="button" value="Example Button">
</form>
</body>
</html>
```

Firstname:

Peter

Lastname:

Griffin

Example Button

Figure 28.5

Section VI
Conclusion

CHAPTER 29

CSS DON'T

Here is one technology you should try to avoid when using CSS.

Internet Explorer Behaviors

What is it? Internet Explorer 5 introduced behaviors. **Behaviors** are a way to add behaviors to HTML elements with the use of CSS styles.

Why avoid it? The behavior attribute is only supported by Internet Explorer.

What to use instead? Use JavaScript and the HTML DOM instead. Learn more in *Learn JavaScript and AJAX with w3schools.*

Example 1—Mouseover Highlight

The following HTML file has a `<style>` element that defines a behavior for the `<h1>` element. Figure 29.1 shows the results of this code, as it appears in IE. The figure has been modified to show the effect of the mouseover.

```
<html>
<head>
<style type="text/css">
   h1 { behavior:url(behave.htc) }
</style>
</head>

<body>
<h1>Mouse over me!!!</h1>
</body>
</html>
```

The XML document behave.htc follows.

Example (IE 5+ Only)

The behavior file contains a JavaScript and event handlers for the elements.

```
<attach for="element" event="onmouseover" handler="hig_lite"
   />
<attach for="element" event="onmouseout" handler="low_lite"
   />

<script type="text/javascript">
   function hig_lite()
   {
      element.style.color='red';
   }

   function low_lite()
   {
      element.style.color='blue';
   }
</script>
```

> # Mouse over me!!!
>
> > ## Mouse over me!!!

Figure 29.1

Example 2—Typewriter Simulation

The following HTML file has a `<style>` element that defines a behavior for elements with an `id` of `typing`. Figure 29.2 shows the results of this behavior, as it appears in IE.

```
<html>
<head>
<style type="text/css">
   #typing
   {
      behavior:url(behave_typing.htc);
      font-family:"courier new";
   }
```

```
</style>
</head>

<body>
<span id="typing" speed="100">IE5 introduced DHTML
  behaviors. Behaviors are a way to add DHTML functionality
  to HTML elements with the ease of CSS.<br />
<br />
How do behaviors work?<br />
By using XML we can link behaviors to any element in a Web
  page and manipulate that element.</p>
</span>
</body>
</html>
```

The XML document typing.htc is shown here:

Example (IE 5+ Only)

```
<attach for="window" event="onload" handler="beginTyping" />
<method name="type" />

<script type="text/javascript">
   var i,text1,text2,textLength,t;

   function beginTyping()
   {
      i=0;
      text1=element.innerText;
      textLength=text1.length;
      element.innerText="";
      text2="";
      t=window.setInterval(element.id+".type()",speed);
   }

   function type()
   {
      text2=text2+text1.substring(i,i+1);
      element.innerText=text2;
      i=i+1;
      if (i==textLength)
```

(continued)

(continued)

```
            {
                clearInterval(t);
            }
        }
    </script>
```

```
IE5 introduced DHTML behaviors. Behaviors are
a way to add DHTML functionality to HTML
elements with the ease of CSS.

How do behaviors work?
By using XML we can link behaviors to any el
```

Figure 29.2

The behavior makes the text come up one letter at a time on the page as if you are watching as it is typed.

CHAPTER 30

YOU HAVE LEARNED CSS...NOW WHAT?

CSS Summary

This tutorial has taught you how to create style sheets to control the style and layout of multiple Web sites at once.

You have learned how to use CSS to add backgrounds, format text, add and format borders, and specify padding and margins of elements.

You have also learned how to position an element, control the visibility and size of an element, set the shape of an element, place an element behind another, and add special effects to some selectors, such as links.

For more information on CSS, please visit the w3schools Web site at www.w3schools.com/css, and take a look at the CSS Examples and CSS Reference sections.

Now You Know CSS, What's Next?

The next step is to learn JavaScript and AJAX.

JavaScript and AJAX

JavaScript and AJAX can make your Web site more dynamic.

A static Web site is nice when you just want to show flat content, but a dynamic Web site can react to events and allow user interaction.

JavaScript is the most popular scripting language on the Internet, and it works with all major browsers. AJAX is a new way to use existing standards based on JavaScript and HTTP requests.

If you want to learn more about JavaScript and AJAX, please read *Learn JavaScript and AJAX with w3schools*.

CSS PROPERTY GROUPS

 If you visit this reference on the w3schools Web site, www.w3schools.com/ css/css_reference.asp, you will find links for each item in the "Property" column that point to syntax, examples, browser support, and so on.

The CSS column indicates in which CSS version the property is defined (CSS1 or CSS2).

Background Properties

> For more information about background properties, see Chapter 4, "Styling Backgrounds."

Property	Description	CSS
background	Sets all the background properties in one declaration	1
background-attachment	Sets whether a background image is fixed or scrolls with the rest of the page	1
background-color	Sets the background color of an element	1
background-image	Sets the background image for an element	1
background-position	Sets the starting position of a background image	1
background-repeat	Sets how a background image will be repeated	1

Border and Outline Properties

> For more information about border and outline properties, see Chapter 11, "CSS Border," and Chapter 12, "CSS Outlines."

Property	Description	CSS
border	Sets all the border properties in one declaration	1
border-bottom	Sets all the bottom border properties in one declaration	1
border-bottom-color	Sets the color of the bottom border	2
border-bottom-style	Sets the style of the bottom border	2
border-bottom-width	Sets the width of the bottom border	1

Property	Description	CSS
border-color	Sets the color of the four borders	1
border-left	Sets all the left border properties in one declaration	1
border-left-color	Sets the color of the left border	2
border-left-style	Sets the style of the left border	2
border-left-width	Sets the width of the left border	1
border-right	Sets all the right border properties in one declaration	1
border-right-color	Sets the color of the right border	2
border-right-style	Sets the style of the right border	2
border-right-width	Sets the width of the right border	1
border-style	Sets the style of the four borders	1
border-top	Sets all the top border properties in one declaration	1
border-top-color	Sets the color of the top border	2
border-top-style	Sets the style of the top border	2
border-top-width	Sets the width of the top border	1
border-width	Sets the width of the four borders	1
outline	Sets all the outline properties in one declaration	2
outline-color	Sets the color of an outline	2
outline-style	Sets the style of an outline	2
outline-width	Sets the width of an outline	2

Dimension Properties

For more information about dimension properties, see Chapter 16, "CSS Dimension."

Property	Description	CSS
height	Sets the height of an element	1
max-height	Sets the maximum height of an element	2
max-width	Sets the maximum width of an element	2
min-height	Sets the minimum height of an element	2
min-width	Sets the minimum width of an element	2
width	Sets the width of an element	1

Font Properties

 For more information about font properties, see Chapter 6, "Styling Fonts."

Property	Description	CSS
font	Sets all the font properties in one declaration	1
font-family	Specifies the font family for text	1
Property	Description	CSS
font-size	Specifies the font size of text	1
font-style	Specifies the font style for text	1
font-variant	Specifies whether a text should be displayed in a small-caps font	1
font-weight	Specifies the weight of a font	1

Generated Content Properties

 For more information about content properties, see Chapter 22, "CSS Pseudo-Elements."

Property	Description	CSS
content	Used with the :before and :after pseudo-elements, to insert generated content	2
counter-increment	Increments one or more counters	2
counter-reset	Creates or resets one or more counters	2
quotes	Sets the type of quotation marks for embedded quotations	2

List Properties

 For more information about list properties, see Chapter 7, "Styling Lists."

Property	Description	CSS
list-style	Sets all the properties for a list in one declaration	1
list-style-image	Specifies an image as the list-item marker	1
list-style-position	Specifies if the list-item markers should appear inside or outside the content flow	1
list-style-type	Specifies the type of list-item marker	1

Margin Properties

For more information about margin properties, see Chapter 13: "CSS Margin."

Property	Description	CSS
margin	Sets all the margin properties in one declaration	1
margin-bottom	Sets the bottom margin of an element	1
margin-left	Sets the left margin of an element	1
Property	Description	CSS
margin-right	Sets the right margin of an element	1
margin-top	Sets the top margin of an element	1

Padding Properties

For more information about padding properties, see "Chapter 14: CSS Padding."

Property	Description	CSS
padding	Sets all the padding properties in one declaration	1
padding-bottom	Sets the bottom padding of an element	1
padding-left	Sets the left padding of an element	1
padding-right	Sets the right padding of an element	1
padding-top	Sets the top padding of an element	1

Positioning Properties

For more information about positioning properties, see Chapter 18, "CSS Positioning."

Property	Description	CSS
bottom	Sets the bottom margin edge for a positioned box	2
clear	Specifies which sides of an element where other floating elements are not allowed	1
clip	Clips an absolutely positioned element	2
cursor	Specifies the type of cursor to be displayed	2
display	Specifies the type of box an element should generate	1
float	Specifies whether or not a box should float	1
left	Sets the left margin edge for a positioned box	2

(continued)

(continued)

Property	Description	CSS
overflow	Specifies what happens if content overflows an element's box	2
position	Specifies the type of positioning for an element	2
right	Sets the right margin edge for a positioned box	2
top	Sets the top margin edge for a positioned box	2
visibility	Specifies whether or not an element is visible	2
z-index	Sets the stack order of an element	2

Print Properties

For more information about print properties, see Chapter 27, "Media Types."

Property	Description	CSS
orphans	Sets the minimum number of lines that must be left at the bottom of a page when a page break occurs inside an element	2
page-break-after	Sets the page-breaking behavior after an element	2
page-break-before	Sets the page-breaking behavior before an element	2
page-break-inside	Sets the page-breaking behavior inside an element	2
widows	Sets the minimum number of lines that must be left at the top of a page when a page break occurs inside an element	2

Table Properties

For more information about table properties, see Chapter 9, "Styling Tables."

Property	Description	CSS
border-collapse	Specifies whether or not table borders should be collapsed	2
border-spacing	Specifies the distance between the borders of adjacent cells	2
caption-side	Specifies the placement of a table caption	2
empty-cells	Specifies whether or not to display borders and background on empty cells in a table	2
table-layout	Sets the layout algorithm to be used for a table	2

Text Properties

For more information about text properties, see Chapter 5, "Styling Text."

Property	Description	CSS
color	Sets the color of text	1
direction	Specifies the text direction/writing direction	2
letter-spacing	Increases or decreases the space between characters in a text	1
line-height	Sets the line height	1
text-align	Specifies the horizontal alignment of text	1
text-decoration	Specifies the decoration added to text	1
text-indent	Specifies the indentation of the first line in a text-block	1
text-shadow	Specifies the shadow effect added to text	2
text-transform	Controls the capitalization of text	1
unicode-bidi		2
vertical-align	Sets the vertical alignment of an element	1
white-space	Specifies how white-space inside an element is handled	1
word-spacing	Increases or decreases the space between words in a text	1

CSS Pseudo-Classes/Elements

For more information about background properties, see Chapter 21, "CSS Pseudo-Classes," and Chapter 22, "CSS Pseudo-Elements."

Property	Description	CSS
:active	Adds a style to an element that is activated	1
:after	Adds content after an element	2
:before	Adds content before an element	2
:first-child	Adds a style to an element that is the first child of another element	2
:first-letter	Adds a style to the first character of a text	1
:first-line	Adds a style to the first line of a text	1
:focus	Adds a style to an element that has keyboard input focus	2
:hover	Adds a style to an element when you mouse over it	1
:lang	Adds a style to an element with a specific lang attribute	2
:link	Adds a style to an unvisited link	1
:visited	Adds a style to a visited link	1

Aural Style Sheets

Aural style sheets use a combination of speech synthesis and sound effects to enable the user to listen to information instead of reading information. The aural presentation converts the document to plain text and feeds this to a screen reader (a program that reads all the characters on the screen).

 For more information about CSS Aural Style Sheets visit the CSS Aural Reference page on the w3schools Web site, at www.w3schools.com/css/css_ref_aural.asp.

CSS WEB SAFE FONT COMBINATIONS

Commonly Used Font Combinations

The font-family property should hold several font names as a "fallback" system, to ensure maximum compatibility between browsers/operating systems. If the browser does not support the first font, it tries the next font.

Start with the font you want and end with a generic family to let the browser pick a similar font in the generic family, if no other fonts are available:

Example

```
p{font-family:"Times New Roman", Times, serif}
```

Following are some commonly used font combinations, organized by generic family.

Serif Fonts

font-family	Example text
Georgia, serif	**This is a heading** This is a paragraph
"Palatino Linotype", "Book Antiqua", Palatino, serif	**This is a heading** This is a paragraph
"Times New Roman", Times, serif	**This is a heading** This is a paragraph

Sans Serif Fonts

font-family	Example text
Arial, Helvetica, sans-serif	**This is a heading** This is a paragraph
"Arial Black", Gadget, sans-serif	**This is a heading** **This is a paragraph**
"Comic Sans MS", cursive, sans-serif	**This is a heading** This is a paragraph
Impact, Charcoal, sans-serif	**This is a heading** **This is a paragraph**
"Lucida Sans Unicode", "Lucida Grande", sans-serif	This is a heading This is a paragraph
Tahoma, Geneva, sans-serif	**This is a heading** This is a paragraph
"Trebuchet MS", Helvetica, sans-serif	**This is a heading** This is a paragraph
Verdana, Geneva, sans-serif	**This is a heading** This is a paragraph

Monospace Fonts

font-family	Example text
"Courier New", Courier, monospace	**This is a heading** This is a paragraph
"Lucida Console", Monaco, monospace	This is a heading This is a paragraph

CSS Units

Measurement Values

Unit	Description
%	percentage
in	inch
cm	centimeter
mm	millimeter
em	1em is equal to the current font size. 2em means 2 times the size of the current font. For example, if an element is displayed with a font of 12 pt, then '2em' is 24 pt. The 'em' is a very useful unit in CSS, because it can adapt automatically to the font that the reader uses
ex	one ex is the x-height of a font (x-height is usually about half the font size)
pt	point (1 pt is the same as 1/72 inch)
pc	pica (1 pc is the same as 12 points)
px	pixels (a dot on the computer screen)

Color Values

Value	Description
color_name	A color name (for example, red)
rgb(x,x,x)	An RGB value (for example, rgb(255,0,0))
rgb(x%, x%, x%)	An RGB percentage value (for example, rgb(100%,0%,0%))
#rrggbb	A HEX number (for example, #ff0000)

CSS COLORS

Colors are displayed combining **red, green,** and **blue** light.

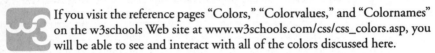

If you visit the reference pages "Colors," "Colorvalues," and "Colornames" on the w3schools Web site at www.w3schools.com/css/css_colors.asp, you will be able to see and interact with all of the colors discussed here.

For more information about using color, see Chapter 4, "Styling Backgrounds," Chapter 5, "Styling Text," and Chapter 11, "CSS Border."

Color Values

CSS colors are defined using a hexadecimal (hex) notation for the combination of Red, Green, and Blue color values (RGB). The lowest value that can be given to one of the light sources is 0 (hex 00). The highest value is 255 (hex FF).

Hex values are written as three double-digit numbers, starting with a # sign.

The combination of Red, Green and Blue values from 0 to 255 gives a total of more than 16 million colors to play with (256 × 256 × 256).

Most modern monitors are capable of displaying at least 16,384 colors.

Gray colors are displayed using an equal amount of power to all of the light sources.

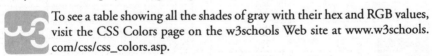

To see a table showing all the shades of gray with their hex and RGB values, visit the CSS Colors page on the w3schools Web site at www.w3schools. com/css/css_colors.asp.

Web Standard Color Names

The World Wide Web Consortium (W3C) has listed 16 valid color names for HTML and CSS.

▶▶ Aqua	▶▶ Fuchsia	▶▶ Lime
▶▶ Black	▶▶ Gray	▶▶ Maroon
▶▶ Blue	▶▶ Green	▶▶ Navy

▶▶ Olive   ▶▶ Silver   ▶▶ White

▶▶ Purple   ▶▶ Teal   ▶▶ Yellow

▶▶ Red

If you want to use other colors, you should specify their hex value.

Cross-Browser Color Names

A collection of nearly 150 color names are supported by all major browsers.

NOTE The names listed in this section are not a part of the W3C Web standard. If you want valid HTML or CSS use the hex values instead.

Table 6.1 provides a list of the color names that are supported by all major browsers.

Table 6.1

Color Name	HEX	Color Name	HEX
AliceBlue	#F0F8FF	DarkKhaki	#BDB76B
AntiqueWhite	#FAEBD7	DarkMagenta	#8B008B
Aqua	#00FFFF	DarkOliveGreen	#556B2F
Aquamarine	#7FFFD4	DarkOrange	#FF8C00
Azure	#F0FFFF	DarkOrchid	#9932CC
Beige	#F5F5DC	DarkRed	#8B0000
Bisque	#FFE4C4	DarkSalmon	#E9967A
Black	#000000	DarkSeaGreen	#8FBC8F
BlanchedAlmond	#FFEBCD	DarkSlateBlue	#483D8B
Blue	#0000FF	DarkSlateGray	#2F4F4F
BlueViolet	#8A2BE2	DarkTurquoise	#00CED1
Brown	#A52A2A	DarkViolet	#9400D3
BurlyWood	#DEB887	DeepPink	#FF1493
CadetBlue	#5F9EA0	DeepSkyBlue	#00BFFF
Chartreuse	#7FFF00	DimGray	#696969
Chocolate	#D2691E	DodgerBlue	#1E90FF
Coral	#FF7F50	FireBrick	#B22222
CornflowerBlue	#6495ED	FloralWhite	#FFFAF0
Cornsilk	#FFF8DC	ForestGreen	#228B22
Crimson	#DC143C	Fuchsia	#FF00FF
Cyan	#00FFFF	Gainsboro	#DCDCDC
DarkBlue	#00008B	GhostWhite	#F8F8FF
DarkCyan	#008B8B	Gold	#FFD700
DarkGoldenRod	#B8860B	Goldenrod	#DAA520
DarkGray	#A9A9A9	Gray	#808080
DarkGreen	#006400	Green	#008000

(continued)

(continued)

Color Name	HEX	Color Name	HEX
GreenYellow	#ADFF2F	OldLace	#FDF5E6
HoneyDew	#F0FFF0	Olive	#808000
HotPink	#FF69B4	OliveDrab	#6B8E23
IndianRed	#CD5C5C	Orange	#FFA500
Indigo	#4B0082	OrangeRed	#FF4500
Ivory	#FFFFF0	Orchid	#DA70D6
Khaki	#F0E68C	PaleGoldenrod	#EEE8AA
Lavender	#E6E6FA	PaleGreen	#98FB98
LavenderBlush	#FFF0F5	PaleTurquoise	#AFEEEE
LawnGreen	#7CFC00	PaleVioletRed	#D87093
LemonChiffon	#FFFACD	PapayaWhip	#FFEFD5
LightBlue	#ADD8E6	PeachPuff	#FFDAB9
LightCoral	#F08080	Peru	#CD853F
LightCyan	#E0FFFF	Pink	#FFC0CB
LightGoldenrodYellow	#FAFAD2	Plum	#DDA0DD
LightGray	#D3D3D3	PowderBlue	#B0E0E6
LightGreen	#90EE90	Purple	#800080
LightPink	#FFB6C1	Red	#FF0000
LightSalmon	#FFA07A	RosyBrown	#BC8F8F
LightSeaGreen	#20B2AA	RoyalBlue	#4169E1
LightSkyBlue	#87CEFA	SaddleBrown	#8B4513
LightSlateGray	#778899	Salmon	#FA8072
LightSteelBlue	#B0C4DE	SandyBrown	#F4A460
LightYellow	#FFFFE0	SeaGreen	#2E8B57
Lime	#00FF00	SeaShell	#FFF5EE
LimeGreen	#32CD32	Sienna	#A0522D
Linen	#FAF0E6	Silver	#C0C0C0
Magenta	#FF00FF	SkyBlue	#87CEEB
Maroon	#800000	SlateBlue	#6A5ACD
MediumAquaMarine	#66CDAA	SlateGray	#708090
MediumBlue	#0000CD	Snow	#FFFAFA
MediumOrchid	#BA55D3	SpringGreen	#00FF7F
MediumPurple	#9370D8	SteelBlue	#4682B4
MediumSeaGreen	#3CB371	Tan	#D2B48C
MediumSlateBlue	#7B68EE	Teal	#008080
MediumSpringGreen	#00FA9A	Thistle	#D8BFD8
MediumTurquoise	#48D1CC	Tomato	#FF6347
MediumVioletRed	#C71585	Turquoise	#40E0D0
MidnightBlue	#191970	Violet	#EE82EE
MintCream	#F5FFFA	Wheat	#F5DEB3
MistyRose	#FFE4E1	White	#FFFFFF
Moccasin	#FFE4B5	WhiteSmoke	#F5F5F5
NavajoWhite	#FFDEAD	Yellow	#FFFF00
Navy	#000080	YellowGreen	#9ACD32